CITY FAITH

Following Jesus in Expensive,

Transient, Secular Places

by Jared Kirk

D1531138

"This book is the resource I didn't realize was missing until I read it. A new generation of Christians has arrived in urban areas, and a new set of faith-related problems and solutions along with it. This work truly meets the moment. If you're a Christian in your twenties or thirties living in a major city, this book is going to read your mail—and then help you sort it out."

GARRETT RABURN Lead Church Planter,
Mission City Church, NYC

"The most significant mission fields in our nation are large metropolitan areas. City Faith equips believers in the challenges of living in and reaching a city for Christ. This book is not theory; it is practical wisdom from someone who has experienced the ups and downs of living out his faith in the heart of the city."

MAC LAKE Author, *The Multiplication Effect*
Founder, The Multiply Group

"Reading City Faith made me think of the popular quote 'Do Hard Things.' Jared and Heather chose to do a hard thing by planting a church in downtown Boston. They stayed committed to that hard thing, and in the perseverance learned the hard faith lessons that metro living teaches. Their perseverance has resulted in the discovery of practical, biblical, motivating insights that will help your faith thrive in the city."

BRIAN PHIPPS Author, *Find Your Place*
Founder, Disciples Made

"The gospel births in us a relentless optimism about what God can accomplish in even the briefest of moments or shortest of seasons. City Faith was written for those who are "just passing through" the city but are open to seeing Christ make the most of their time. It is the book I'll hand to anyone I meet who anticipates having just two or three years with us ... for their good, and for the good of our church."

MATTHEW KRUSE – Lead Pastor,
Seven Mile Road, Melrose, MA
Author, *What Church Can Be*

"Jared has put together a helpful, readable, and practical guide to navigating city life by making wise, godly decisions. If you're finding you way into a city, find your way into this book."

ADAM MABRY Lead Pastor, Aletheia Church
Author, *Stop Taking Sides*

"If you live in the city and are wondering how you can be transformed and help being transformation through your faith in Jesus, City Faith is the catalyst you've been hoping for."

ERIC GAMERO Lead Pastor, The Local Church

This outstanding book should be included in the "survival pack" for any young man or woman moving into the city for the first time. For those already in the city, the stories and rich insight in this book will awaken both personal flourishing and increased impact. I have two daughters who are about to graduate college and launch into their next season, which may land them in a new city. As I read City Faith I thought, "Maddie and Whitney need to read this. I'm going to buy them both a copy."

ROB WEGNER Director, The Kansas City Underground, Author, *Find Your Place: Locating Your Calling Through Gifts, Passions, and Story*, *Made for More*, and *The Starfish and The Spirit: Unleashing the Leadership Potential of Churches and Organizations*

FREE DOWNLOAD

- Discussion Guide

- Recorded Meditation Scriptures
  for Urban Christians

- Bonus Gift

Get your free downloads at
www.JaredKirk.com/CityFaithBonus

This book is dedicated to all the pastors and missionaries who went to the hard places to grow God's family

TABLE OF CONTENTS

INTRODUCTION

Brittany arrived in Boston, where I pastor Renewal Church, to take a job in marketing. She is the kind of person likely to open her own marketing firm someday. She is driven, kind, quiet in crowds, personable in smaller groups, and she carries herself with an athleticism she earned playing tennis in West Palm Beach, Florida.

When I met Brittany, she was coasting in her faith. She had plenty of exposure to Christianity, but it wasn't a grounding foundation in her life. She started attending church and, at first, was a passive witness. She would come, sit, watch, and listen. She didn't engage deeply, which made sense because she wasn't planning on being in Boston very long. Her focus was on her career, and her faith was on cruise control.

One of the amazing things about God is that He cares for you whether you care much for Him or not. And, out of God's great love for Brittany, He grabbed her attention through some difficult family circumstances. Those difficulties became the catalyst for profound change in her life. She stepped out of the anonymity of the crowd into the bright lights of the church community. She built relationships that are still strong years later. She hosted a Bible study in her apartment. She started to grow spiritually. We watched as her faith brought peace and hope in the midst of those strained family relationships. We marveled as a natural leader in the marketplace, skilled at making money, became a spiritual leader skilled at helping other people grow.

Then one day, she had to leave our church and our lives, just like that. We were heartbroken by her departure because, when you're losing a friend to distance, it's still a loss. People tend to come and go at a breakneck pace in the city.

When Brittany left our church, I was concerned for her growing faith. Would it survive the loss of community and support? Would it survive her move to New York City? It turns out I was worried for nothing. She connected with a church in that city, and her faith continued to grow tremendously. She was baptized. She became a small group leader. She lived with conviction when questioned by friends and family. She is making an impact for Christ in one of the largest global cities of the world, and at the same time, Christ is impacting her life in hugely beneficial ways.

I know that Brittany's story is not typical. Most people who live in cities don't embrace faith deeply. However, I do know for certain that Brittany's story could be your story. The pressure from the city might crush your faith or it might turn it into something far more precious than gold.

This book was written for the hundreds of thousands of people who move into cities every year for a multitude of reasons. It is about how to write a better story for your life in any metropolitan area. It's about how to stop coasting and start growing spiritually during your urban adventure. It's about how to leverage the small amount of time you have in the city to grow spiritually so that you leave town deeply impacted by God and ready to bring the hope and freedom of Jesus with you wherever you go next.

Each chapter in this book explores a decision you must make for spiritual growth, but it does so through the lens of expensive, transient, secular life in the city. I have learned these principles by leading wave after wave of people through their time in Boston at an incredibly ordinary yet unique place called Renewal Church in the downtown area. It's ordinary because we are focused on glorifying God (showing who He is and what He's like) and making disciples (followers of Jesus). It's unique because, as a center-city church, we have had a front row seat witnessing how an urban context affects people of faith. Boston is the crucible in which I've learned to help new people, who may only be in the city between ten and thirty-six months, connect quickly and effectively into a life-giving relationship with God and with a local church.

To claim that I've discovered these principles on my own is arrogance. I've been a part of a collective of city church planters in Boston for years now—our group text is called "City Guys"—and each pastor has contributed a new perspective on how Christians grow spiritually and overcome the barriers the city throws at them. This group of pastors is a brotherhood dedicated to helping people in the city grow in their love for Jesus, and it's one of the reasons God is doing a new thing in the city of Boston.

- JD Mangrum taught me what it looks like to be knee deep in my neighborhood.
- Charlie Dunn taught me how to apply the gospel to the disappointments of the hurting.
- Josh Wyatt taught me what steadfastness can accomplish over a decade in the city.
- Steven Castello taught me how to create unity from diversity in the local church.
- Jonathan Moseley taught me how to connect with students from international backgrounds.

So this book is the product of the collected wisdom of a team of pastors helping cynical, secular people become passionate followers of Jesus in an urban environment. (If you one day feel like God is leading you to be a part of the brotherhood, hit me up, I'll get you connected.)

Our City Guys have been working in the metropolis for years now, and we consistently see people at all levels of faith struggle with the unique challenges of living in the city. The loneliness, the transience, the distraction, and the costs are all barriers many of them face in living out their faith and their dreams.

Most people who come to the city have dreams about meeting that special someone, hitting financial goals, and furthering personal development, but the city brings a layer of complexity to accomplishing these goals. I've seen many people struggle to live a life of faith and move forward while in the city, but I've also encountered incredible individuals who have grown tremendously. Through serving those of the city of

Boston, I've distilled things down to the decisions you must make to thrive during your time in an urban environment and the barriers you are likely to encounter along the way. I want to share what I've learned with you.

We're going to cover the decisions you can make to grow spiritually in the city; things that tend to affect urban professionals and pre-professionals like:

- Developing the kind of faith that survives the distractions of the city.
- Making a difference in your city when you don't plan to stay for a lifetime.
- Living generously when your housing is 50 percent of your income.
- Building healthy relationships that last beyond your time in the city.
- Navigating singleness in a godly way.

This book is for you if you find faith challenging in the city. The distractions, the diversions, and the loss of support structures may have made it tough for you to connect. Maybe you feel like you should find a church, but it's been a couple months or a couple years and you just haven't connected with one yet. This book is also for you if you are about to start your urban adventure (or urban college adventure) and you want to be spiritually prepared. Lastly, if you are in a highly transient profession, like the military, I believe this book will still be incredibly helpful, even if you don't live in a city. You all deserve excellent resources for city living.

If this book turns out to be helpful to you, would you let me know personally at Jared@JaredKirk.com? You can also email me if you are struggling with faith in the city. I want to pray for you, and I want you to find your people, in your city, wherever God has placed you.

Blessings,

Pastor Jared Kirk

Ory lived in the smallest apartment I've ever seen. It was good, therefore, that Ory was one of the smallest people I've ever met. He was 5'2" with dress shoes on, and he always wore dress shoes. He had impeccable sartorial taste, but his style extended to all of life. He was the kind of man who wore a pocket square when he wasn't attending a wedding, and he even picked his bicycle for its style.

Ory was from Indonesia but was ethnically Chinese. Since he was the first-born, his father had imparted to him a sense of paternalism that wasn't overbearing in Ory. He would often order at restaurants on behalf of the whole table. It was endearing to watch him take the lead so effortlessly, then give it back in another context.

When our paths crossed, he was going to a church in the Brookline area near Boston. It was in an expensive part of town, but Ory was working for one of the Big Four accounting firms, and he could afford it. Christianity had entered his life early through a Christian school his parents had him attend, but personal faith would be quite a way off for him. It wouldn't be until his thirties, after an incident with a car accident, a praying nurse, and what can only be described as a divine encounter, that he began to believe. Faith was present in his life, but when I met him in Brookline years later, he was coasting spiritually.

I can only speculate why. Perhaps it was the focus on financial accumulation which the city tends to amplify. Perhaps it was the distractions the city offered. Perhaps it was the lack of accountability which the distance from family facilitates. Or perhaps it was the unhealthy relationships that grew out of an extended singleness not yet yielded to God. Whatever it was, Ory's spiritual growth was limited.

Until one day it wasn't. I'm not sure what shifted internally for him, but it was clear that, one day, Ory decided he needed to get serious about growing spiritually during his time in the city. He started serving at the start-up church I was launching. He began investing in a healthy relationship with a Christian couple named Scott and Ashley. Additionally, he made some very significant shifts in his connections with others, exchanging unhealthy dating relationships for God-honoring relationships. God seemed real and present to him, and he was a part of our life, our world, and our community. He was loved.

So we were devastated when his long-term work visa was not renewed. His employer, with whom he had worked for years, had no interest in sponsoring his green card. He had been in the U.S. for over a decade and had built a life here, but now he was going home to Indonesia. As his friend and pastor, I was nervous about his move at first. I wanted him to continue on this spiritual path that had brought so much freedom and peace into his life. I realized soon after the move that my fears had been unfounded.

I learned later that Ory's faith in Jesus was thriving in Indonesia, which is the largest Muslim country in the world by population. He began helping an old friend with a Christian ministry. Before long, he met a woman who loved Jesus even more than he did. They got married, and these days there are two even smaller versions of Ory running around. Ory's investment in spiritual growth for about two years in Boston has paid dividends for a decade.

ARE YOU WAITING FOR WHAT'S NEXT?

Ory's story is an invitation to answer an important question during your time in the city, and it's the question that lies at the heart of this book.

Are you waiting for what's next or are you actively preparing for it?

Chances are you have come to the city for both a purpose and for a season. You have come for a specific reason—education, career, or opportunity.

To achieve this purpose, you have likely come for a season—until you make partner, until you graduate, until you get a better offer. The intense focus of the purpose which drew you to the city and the limited time you expect to commit to living in it can cause you to commit an error that can be fatal to your spiritual life: coasting.

When you believe you are only going to be somewhere for a year or two, why get deeply involved? Why try to build relationships with people you will leave? Why not wait until you are in a more stable position? Thinking like this encourages you to coast spiritually. You are waiting for what's next instead of preparing for it.

But not everyone makes this error. In my years in the city, I've seen a small but substantial minority who refuse to coast and instead choose to grow spiritually during their time in the urban landscape. Decide to grow spiritually during your time in the city. Prepare for what's next.

WHAT'S NEXT

When you think about what comes after your time in the city, you probably think about *what* you will be doing. You'll get a promotion, go on tour, or land that dream job. But I want you to think for a moment about *where* you will end up after your short stint in the city.

Maybe you will "go big", which is to say, you will head to another large, global city. People from my church currently live and work in Hong Kong, London, Johannesburg, Toronto, Nairobi, Medellin, and New York City, to name a few. The unlucky ones get sent to Cincinnati. You may never have considered this, but you have an opportunity to impact the global cities of the world in a positive way by bringing the hope of Jesus with you wherever you go. Are you waiting for this to happen or actively preparing for it?

Or perhaps you will "go home". Going home means heading back to where you came from, wherever that may be. After all, your family might be weird, but they're *your* family. You may be married and have a dream to live near your parents and have children. This might be in a city, but it might be in Macon, Georgia or Fairbanks, Alaska. When you go home, you have an opportunity to bring the freedom of Jesus with you to those people you love so much. Are you coasting in the city or growing spiritually to be ready for that moment?

Lastly, some of you will be surprised that God is leading you to "go long". Maybe part of your heart will call you home and part of your heart will long for greater adventure, but you will sense God leading you to stay in the city long-term. If your two years unexpectedly becomes ten, you don't want to regret how long you waited to bring the joy of Jesus to your city

So again, are you waiting for what's next or are you preparing for what's next?

THE REAL DANGER OF COASTING

The question of whether you are coasting or growing is not only about what's next, it is also about your soul today.

When Jesus was summarizing and simplifying spiritual pursuit, He shared a word picture to help us grasp the way to eternal life.

> *"Enter through the narrow gate. For wide is the gate and broad is the road that leads to destruction, and many enter through it. But small is the gate and narrow the road that leads to life, and only a few find it" (Matt. 7:13-14 NIV).*

According to Jesus, floating along with everyone else spiritually leads you to places you don't want to go. He describes a wide path, full of people, heading for disaster. "Destruction" is the word He uses for the destination of the path most people are walking. We know from Jesus's other teachings that it's a path marked by apathy rather than passion and self-promotion rather than self-denial. All you have to do to end up in "destination destruction" is to coast along with everyone else on the path.

On certain beautiful summer days in Boston, the city closes down specific streets to car traffic. Throngs of people fill the streets, all headed in the same direction, all aiming for the same destination: Fenway Park, home of the Red Sox. If you want to arrive at Fenway Park on one of these magnificent summer days, all you have to do is float along with the crowds and you will arrive at this common destination.

If you are coasting along with everyone else, you'll end up at the same destination as everyone else. But, on the positive side, if you pursue the narrow path tread by few, it leads to eternal life. What characterizes this walk on the narrow path? Well, we know that it's less well-travelled, but there's more, and Jesus tells us a couple of verses later:

"Ask and it will be given to you; seek and you will find; knock and the door will be opened to you. For everyone who asks receives; the one who seeks finds; and to the one who knocks, the door will be opened" (Matt. 7:7 NIV).

The road to life is a road in pursuit of God and His truth. It's a life of seeking. There might be more to salvation than seeking, but there certainly isn't less. The narrow path is a life of spiritual growth. It's the opposite of a life on cruise-control. It is the active search for God that leads to growth.

GROWTH IN THE CITY

If you don't have some kind of growth mindset, the urban environment will eat you alive. Here are some of the most common areas for personal growth in the city:

- Educational/Intellectual Growth
- Career Advancement
- Personal Network Expansion
- Cultural Exposure
- Business Development

The question is not whether growth is happening in your life in the city, but whether you will take Jesus's words to heart and decide to grow instead of settling for stagnation in your spiritual life.

URBAN SPIRITUAL GROWTH BARRIERS

Why are we quick to grow in certain areas of life in the city but slow to engage in spiritual growth in an urban environment? I've identified three major barriers.

DISTRACTION

There is money to be made and fun to be had. There are ideas to monetize, talented people to recruit, and passions to pursue. There are microbreweries, speakeasies, and beer-gardens. There are art exhibits, slam poetry readings, and museums. In my city, you can watch the Boston Marathon and the Red Sox on the same day. We have over one million people turn out for a sculling competition every year. That's one million people watching other people row! Distraction makes growth a challenge.

DECEIT

Cities will expose you to a range of ideas you have never encountered before. Some of these ideas will enrich your life, but some of them will be explicitly opposed to what you believe and you will need to reject them. You will experience lies disguised as the truth, vanity disguised as self-care, lust disguised as self-expression, gluttony disguised as self-affirmation, and immodesty disguised as self-respect. The never-ending barrage of deceitful messages makes spiritual progress challenging.

DISTANCE

If you are in a city, you are likely over two hours from your family and childhood friends. The physical distance limits the support that loved ones may have provided in other times. This creates a lack of accountability for your actions since those who know you best are not there to offer immediate counsel. Since spiritual growth tends to happen where you find vulnerability, accountability, and the truth of God's Word, the lack of accountability is a major growth barrier.

A GOD BIGGER THAN THE BARRIERS

One of the most amazing things about having a relationship with God through His son Jesus is that nothing in your life is ever wasted. No difficulty, no pain, no trial is ever without purpose. There is always a resurrection after a death, and there is always a death before a resurrection. Endings always give way to new beginnings when Jesus is at the center of your life. That was the pattern of Jesus's life, after all. First death, then resurrection. First hardship and suffering, then glory.

What this means for you practically in the city is that the exact same things you view as barriers to spiritual growth may end up being the very things God uses to grow your faith. An easy life has rarely produced a remarkable follower of Jesus.

The distraction you face in the city helps to purify your motives. Do you want to be with God or are you just going through the motions? The deceit you encounter can be so overwhelming that it presses you to find better, purer truth in God's Word. The distance that separates you from your support system can cause you to depend more fully on God in your isolation or loneliness and connect with His community. In short, the city may reveal the weaknesses of your spiritual life, but because of the incredible upside-down message of the cross, we can brag about our weaknesses.

"But [God] said to me, 'My grace is sufficient for you, for my power is made perfect in weakness.' Therefore I will boast all the more gladly about my weaknesses, so that Christ's power may rest on me" (2 Cor. 12:9 NIV).

The God the Bible talks about is so wise and powerful that He can use even the things that trip you up spiritually to grow you spiritually. The more your weakness is revealed, the more you realize you need Jesus. The more you realize your need for Jesus and run to Him, the more you are growing toward God. The city is one of the greatest tools God ever invented to grow your faith.

DECIDE TO GROW SPIRITUALLY

You have a decision to make, and it all comes back to the question at the heart of this book.

Are you waiting for what's next or are you preparing for what's next?

When your time in the city is done, you will probably go big, go home, or go long. You need to decide whether you want to step into that next season of your life with a bigger soul and a life more fully yielded to God, ready to bring the hope and freedom of Jesus with you. The great thing about Ory's story is that he is an ordinary man who is making an extraordinary impact for Jesus on the other side of the globe, all because he leveraged two years to stop coasting and start growing spiritually. That could be your story, too.

CHAPTER 2
DECIDE TO FOLLOW

L ike most people, David showed up in the city in pursuit of a dream. He was a talented drummer and musician who was hoping to turn his passion into a career by attending Berklee College of Music.

He grew up completely surrounded by faith. His mom and dad were both deeply involved in a United Methodist Church. He and his sister were a part of the worship team. Belief was a big part of David's background.

David's belief in Jesus wasn't just a family thing; he had a personal belief in Jesus too. He believed all the correct things about Jesus, and he thought that was enough. However, when David moved to the city, the pain in his life slowly increased. There were destructive habits that couldn't be broken.

There were besetting sins that couldn't be overcome. He thought he believed everything he needed to, but the pain was telling a different story. There was knowledge David was missing.

When David started coming to church in the city, he came to Renewal. I want to assure you that Renewal is a very ordinary church. Maybe we are a little friendlier than most (all New Englanders say this to us), but, generally speaking, we are pretty normal. I say this because it wasn't the power of Renewal that changed David's life. It was an encounter with God.

David heard a message on 1 Corinthians 10:13 (NIV) which says this:

"No temptation has overtaken you except what is common to mankind. And God is faithful; he will not let you be tempted beyond what you can bear. But when you are tempted, he will also provide a way out so that you can endure it."

David relayed to me that when this scripture was read, it was as though God reached into David's chest, grabbed his heart, and crushed it in His hand. God became suddenly and overwhelmingly present, and David surrendered his life to Him. He had believed for a long time, but this was the moment he decided to lay down his will for the will of another and surrender his life to God.

What this started was a process of following the way of Jesus. Learning how to manage finances in a godly way. Learning how to lead himself and then lead others. Radically increasing in the amount of self-control in his life. Living a life full of healthy relationships with life-giving friends. Releasing a passion to serve Jesus and his church with the extra flexibility that comes from being single.

Over time, every aspect of David's life changed for the better, and, from my perspective, that is precisely why David's faith flourished in the city when most people's faith tends to whither. David went from believing to following. When he followed, he was blessed. When he was blessed, it increased his desire to follow.

From the outside, David looks like a person with incredible faith, and he is! But he didn't just wake up like that one day. Instead, he practiced the logic of following, blessing, and faith. When you follow, you're blessed. Then your faith to follow grows.

BELIEF

If you think that Christianity is all about belief, you are correct. Jesus himself kept inviting people to believe in Him.

> *"Jesus said to her, 'I am the resurrection and the life. The one who believes in me will live, even though they die'" (John 11:25 NIV).*

So, yes, Jesus invites you to believe in Him.

However, there is a major issue that has shipwrecked the faith of countless people over the centuries. Simply put, when Jesus talked about belief, He meant something very specific. He clearly didn't mean "believe that I exist" because He was talking to a bunch of people who were looking right at him. Nor did he mean "believe I am the Son of God who has miraculous powers" because He was speaking to people who had just watched Him do

35

miracles with their own eyes. He must have meant something like, "believe that I am the one who, if you commit fully to me and my teachings, will lead you to eternal life."

Jesus's invitation to believe in Him is an invitation to lay down your will and live for the will of God. Jesus's invitation to believe in Him is an invitation to follow Him, to participate in a way of life. That's why His earliest followers were called "followers of The Way." It was the way of Jesus, the way to life.

Most churches don't teach this. It's not that they teach heresy, they are just obsessed with getting people to believe the right things rather than to follow Jesus. You may have gone to a class to make sure you believed all the right things. There might have been a cake and a white dress at the end of the class to celebrate. Maybe they gave you a certificate. They probably didn't call it the "demon level belief certificate," but that's what it was.[1]

---

[1] Shout out to Greg Curtis for introducing me to this term.

"You believe that there is one God. Good!
Even the demons believe that—and shudder"
(James 2:19 NIV).

According to James who was Jesus's brother, acknowledgement of existence (what English speakers usually call "belief") is the most common kind of useless faith. If you intellectually agree that Jesus is the sinless Son of God who died for the sins of the world, then you are at the same level of belief as all of hell.

Is that harsh? I mean, it is, but James never really pulls punches. He always lays it on thick so that you get the point. In fact, try reading the letter James wrote (it's called James and you can look in up in the Table of Contents in a Bible) and you'll see what I'm talking about.

But we get the point, don't we? What good is belief if it doesn't change your life? What good does it do you to acknowledge Jesus exists, but not live out His life of love in your friendships? What good does it do to know how radically generous Jesus was to the poor, but not to care about anyone who has material needs?

BELIEF DIES IN THE CITY

The superficial kind of belief that James pointed out—belief that agrees with the mind but doesn't change anything—is likely to whither in the city. The urban environment challenges superficial belief by exposing you to new ideas, surfacing doubts, and causing a loss of cultural capital.

The city offers too many new ideas you've never encountered before. I once met a Zoroastrian at a birthday party in Brookline. There's like 100,000 of them left in the world. They have "fire temples," which admittedly sound way cooler than "churches." She wanted to know the reasons I believe what I believe. There is no confirmation manual to consult in such situations. I went to a Christian graduate school for several years and they never covered explaining the reasons for your belief to a Zoroastrian. If you are asked why you believe what you believe, would you consult your certificate?

Superficial belief also dies in the city because of doubt. Cynicism is uncommonly common among urban people. So many city dwellers are full of doubt that it can raise any doubts you've buried to the surface. Dealing with doubt is a normal part of getting to belief, but unhealthy doubt provides an excuse to ignore God. You will hear doubt vocalized often and this can be a belief killer.

Finally, superficial belief dies in the city because of the loss of cultural capital associated with it. Cultural capital refers to the intangible benefits and advantages within a particular setting. Urban places tend to be progressive politically. In some parts of America, you can actually gain cultural and social capital by attending church, but in large metropolitan areas the opposite can be true. I once knew a man doing post-doctoral research on genetics who told me his co-workers knocked fifteen points off his I.Q. when he told them he was a Christian. That is loss of cultural capital, and it is deadly to unexamined belief. If you believe because everyone else does, what are the chances you will believe when everyone else doesn't?

A BETTER BELIEF

When belief is simply "acknowledging existence" it always dies easy. You believed in Santa, the Easter Bunny, and the Tooth Fairy, and all it took to kill your belief permanently was an authority figure (usually an eight- or nine-year old) telling you they don't exist.

But when belief is *following* Jesus wholeheartedly, your faith is not contingent upon what authority figures say. You experience it personally. You discover how following the way of Jesus changes the way you speak to people you are dating. You observe as your heart changes toward your roommate. You marvel as you are financially provided for despite your extravagant generosity. You experience the peace that goes beyond logic that carries you through difficult situations. You revel in the joy of being set free from destructive habits.

When you trust God enough to follow Him, you are blessed. You'll have a million reasons you've experienced personally to follow Jesus because He has renewed your life.

If your belief is superficial, it will fail to be transformative and will not sustain you through the challenges of city life. But when Jesus invites you to believe in Him, it is the opposite of superficial. He is inviting you into an adventure. It's a dangerous journey of self-denial that eventually ends in death, but since Jesus is in charge, death does not have the final say. In the economy of the kingdom of God, there is always a death before a resurrection.

DECIDING TO FOLLOW

The question for you in the city is *will you follow Jesus?* If you decide not to follow Him, your belief will probably shrink because it is disconnected from the blessings of following. If, however, you decide to follow Jesus's way of life, then each day you will experience a new way in which God blesses you. Your relationships will become healthier, your finances will no longer stress you endlessly, you'll find yourself able to forgive, destructive habits will change, you'll move through grief in a healthy way,

41

and your self-control will increase. And those are just the blessings for today. The greatest blessings are eternal, and you will learn over time that what God can give you today is absolutely nothing compared to the blessings of having your sins forgiven, walking with God moment by moment, or living in God's presence forever.

So let me ask you, where are you on the spectrum of following Jesus? Put an "X" on the graphic below where you would place yourself.

| Exploring | Believing | Growing | Leading |

At some point in your life, you will encounter the cross of Jesus Christ. The Bible says that God loves you so much that He sent His Son to live a perfect life, die on a cross for your sins, and rise from the dead. God did all this because He wanted His kids back, and now He wants a relationship with you. He wants to give you hope and a future and forgiveness and all the other blessings we've talked about.

Where did you put your "X" on the line? A
relationship with God comes when you surrender
your will to the will of the Father, when you believe
Jesus is your forgiver and your leader. It's when you
say, "not my will but thy will be done in my life" and
you decide to live for God's kingdom instead of your
little fiefdom. When that moment comes, you'll
move from intellectual assent to passionate
pursuit. Life will become an adventure of playing
"follow the leader" with Jesus at the front of the
line.

Maybe you're realizing you have some belief, but
truthfully recognize you have been the leader of
your life, not Jesus. Today, I want to invite you to
decide to follow Jesus, to respond to God's
invitation to have a relationship with Him through
His Son, Jesus Christ. You can do that by making this
prayer your own right now:

*Heavenly Father, I know I need you in my life. I'm
sorry about the way I've lived. I know that I'm a
sinner, and I want to live your way, but I need your
help. I need Jesus. I believe that Jesus is the forgiver*

of my sins and the leader of my life. I want to follow Jesus from this day forward. Amen.

When that prayer reverberates in your soul, when you lay hold of that prayer as hope and life, then you start on the road to life in the city and eternal life in heaven. Instead of crushing your faith, the city becomes a tool God uses to grow and stretch you on this great adventure of bringing God's kingdom of justice and peace to your city.

If you're starting a relationship with God today, I want to ask you to do one thing and it is very, very important. You need to plunge your past. Baptism is *the* action step you take to show you are following Jesus. Talk to a pastor at any local church about baptism. Just ask, *"Can I talk to someone about being baptized?"* and every good church in the world will help you grow from there.

FOLLOWING IN THE CITY

The rest of this book is about following Jesus in the city. There are unique challenges to doing so in the city, but amazing Christians have done it and have wisdom to share. If you settle for intellectual assent, you will likely move between forgettable relationships, grow in selfishness, leave in debt, and lose what little belief you have.

Come to think of it, that's what Jesus said about spiritual understanding:

"Whoever has will be given more; whoever does not have, even what they have will be taken from them" (Mark 4:25 NIV).

However, if you dive head-first into the adventure of following Jesus in the city, you will likely form life-long relationships, grow in selflessness, develop disciplined finances, and be able to clearly articulate your faith in an intelligent way. That's what happened in David's life. The God Who Changes Everything became suddenly and unexpectedly present to him, and now his life is different. Think about what you might miss out on if you don't follow that God during your time in the city.

CHAPTER 3
DECIDE TO CONNECT

Your decision to connect with other people in healthy relationships will bear fruit when you need it most. Heather and I have always hosted a small Bible study group in our home of some kind. They are always fun. We've made dozens of friends who now live all over the country that we keep in touch with to this day. Sometimes these groups are interesting. Sometimes we learn new things. Sometimes we just circle up to go through the normal parts of a regular life with an extraordinary God guiding the way. There is, though, one group in particular I will always remember.

Miranda was a part of this group. Miranda is crazy smart, soft-spoken, competent, and loves Jesus. She is quick with a laugh or a smile and just as quick with a Bible verse when the moment strikes. We celebrated with her when she got engaged and again when she got married. I had never been to a Black/Puerto Rican wedding before, and I can legitimately say on behalf of white people everywhere that we need to step up our wedding game. It was a huge surprise to Miranda, and to us, when her marriage started to unravel in the first year due to circumstances beyond her control.

Our group became a special place for all of us. Each week, we would gather together and go through whatever study we were working on, but after the study was over, the real group began. Miranda would update us on her life. We sanctified that living room with our tears together. We prayed with her and for her. When the Bible study ended, the community began.

It was there I learned the true power of community to heal and to help. The healthy, God-honoring relationships that you develop when you make the decision to connect are what support you through the tough times in life. I also learned there is a world of difference between a one-hour Bible study and a community of friends to help you follow Jesus through life.

THE GOAL ISN'T A BIBLE STUDY

Our time with Miranda reminded me that true connection with people often surprises you at unexpected moments. You have to be with people enough so spontaneity can arise, but for most Christians in the city, we are settling for a one-hour Bible study and calling it community. We are looking at a page together, discussing it, and calling it connection. It doesn't work if you aren't fully known and fully loved. It doesn't work if you aren't being real.

You will thrive when you share your life with a few other Christians who help you follow Jesus in the city. This is your band of brothers. This is your squad. The goal can't be a one-hour Bible study. The goal must be biblical community. You need people you can be every part of yourself around. You need people with whom you can go to concerts and talk Jesus, go apple picking and talk about your struggles. It is good to be with people who know what your sins are and care enough to ask you about them; people you will never forget, even when you leave the city.

ONE LONG HORROR MOVIE

In the city, there are several unique barriers to community which need to be addressed and overcome. There are work commitments, transience, and diversity.

The first barrier to community in the city is work commitments. Perhaps you are in the city specifically to get ahead in your career. This creates an environment for you to overwork and for your workplace to overschedule you. Think about accountants working for the Big Four in their first few years and you catch the drift.

In one Bible study group, a man named Augustine would leave work to come to our apartment at 7 p.m. and leave after group to go back to work. He made the group a priority, and no one at his work ever said a word, but he had to manage significant work commitments to attend.

49

The second barrier is that your friends all leave. Friendship in the city can feel like one, long horror movie. It starts off with a squad of friends having a great time together, but one by one they mysteriously disappear. One friend gets separated from the group, they go on a work trip to the suburbs of Atlanta, and before long they are the next one living in a home five times the size of their previous apartment.

That's a bit dramatic, but if you stay for longer than twelve months in a busy urban center, you will know exactly what I'm talking about. Grieving in a godly way for lost relationships is one of the most important skills for living in the city that no one talks about.

The third barrier is diversity. You've probably never thought about this because in American society diversity tends to be prized as an end unto itself. However, it is commonality rather than diversity that forms the natural environment in which community grows. Therefore, to build community among diverse peoples requires cross-cultural competency.

In a city church, you will likely encounter diversity of race, ethnicity, immigration status, sexual orientation, gender identity, economic level, educational attainment, and political viewpoint. That might seem like a lot, but take heart. These are barriers to be overcome, not a solitary confinement sentence for lonely people.

A GOD BIGGER THAN THE BARRIERS

When you follow God in the city, He gives you the strength and skills you need to develop a life-giving community. He also gives you a savior for the times when you fall short.

Cities provide huge crowds of disconnected people hungry for relational connection. You've probably been on some dating apps, so you know it's true. You also know that dating apps are definitely not the best way to build your friend group. When you jump into a church, there will be some kind of group for you to join. In city churches, there are rarely long-term cliques that are impenetrable to newcomers because there are few old-timers. If you join a small group, you are likely to meet other people new to the city who are looking for relational connection, focused on growth, and following Jesus.

That diversity I mentioned as a barrier can obviously enrich your life with interesting relationships. If you want to look at this from a Jesus perspective, you might say that the city provides a never-ending variety of people that you can learn to love well. God's creativity is on display in the people He has made, and living like Jesus means figuring out how to help each one feel loved.

CONNECTING WITH PEOPLE IS LOVING GOD
True connection and community changes you. Your healthy relationships dramatically increase the quality of your life, and even the way you love God changes.

Connecting with people in a healthy way and meeting their needs is how you can show your love for God. I have three kids, and the fastest way to my heart is through my children. People who care for them or give them gifts or help them grow are all people showing their love for me. When we were gathering with Miranda, we were just loving our friend, but I believe God loved those times. As we were loving one of His kids, we were loving Him.

This is great news for people who just don't "feel it" when they go to church. I'm one of those guys. I have the "emotional range of a teaspoon," and this often carries over into my experience of worship.[2] At church, there are usually a few people who sit right up in the front, arms raised, and eyes closed like they are scoring one very long, very quiet touchdown. Or perhaps their arms are only half-way raised with palms up, like they are carrying an invisible television. Or perhaps they are swaying gently to the sound of the music like one of those orange inflatable guys outside of a used car lot. I

---

[2] Having "the emotional range of a teaspoon" is what Hermione accused Ron of in the movie "Harry Potter and the Order of the Phoenix."

struggle to worship like these people. Sometimes my heart is unexpectedly warmed and my awareness of other people's perception melts away, but often I wonder why I don't look like the people in the front row.

What revolutionized my view of worship was a sentence from the Bible that doesn't really seem like it's about worship at all. It's from the first letter we possess from an early follower of Jesus called John and it says this:

"Whoever claims to love God yet hates a brother or sister is a liar. For whoever does not love their brother and sister, whom they have seen, cannot love God, whom they have not seen" (1 John 4:20 NIV).

These sentences very closely equate loving people with loving God. You can't love God and hate His kids. They are a package deal. When you love His children, you are showing your love for Him. That's why when I learned to see Sundays as an opportunity to love people, they came alive for me. I promise that you can find better sermons online than you can at my church, and there are many professionally produced live worship services online, but it's hard to love real people in a virtual space.

In the visible connections between people, the invisible God becomes visible again. It's in the moment you ask, "How are you, really?", and in your joyful but slightly off-key singing of truths about grace, forgiveness, and hope that you know your friends can hear. It's in the decision to sit next to the person who often sits alone, and in the encouragement for the struggling friend. It's in the invitation to brunch and the smile you share at the table. You are loving God in all these moments.

And that person on the front row holding the television? "*Judge not lest ye be judged*" (Matt. 7:1 KJV). Who knows? Maybe they are loving God well, maybe they aren't. In my default assumption that other people are holier than me, I'm usually proved correct. The important thing is that the quality of your love isn't judged by your passion displayed in worship, but in the mercy you show to the people around you.

THE POWER OF PRIORITIES

In the suburbs, schedules mostly are crazy because of soccer practice, play dates, dance classes, and commute times. In the city, your schedule mostly is crazy because of work commitments, work travel, transportation issues, and the lure of a good beer garden. Basically, everyone I know in America is busy no matter where they live. You are going to have to choose to prioritize connection into community or it's not going to happen.

There are significant barriers to building community in the city, but there is an antidote. Like many things in life, it's simple, but not easy. When you make building community a priority in your life, it tends to happen. It's as simple as that. Jesus talked about the power of priorities when He said,

"But seek first his kingdom and his righteousness, and all these things will be given to you as well"
(Matt. 6:33 NIV).

Jesus takes here the law of priorities and applies it spiritually. The law of priorities works like this: when your priorities are right, everything falls into place. When your priorities are wrong, everything falls apart. According to Jesus, life works when you put God first. God provides for you and His kingdom, and His righteousness is given to you. You must love God above all else, and loving God is always loving His kids.

The importance of prioritizing connection with God's people was illustrated powerfully at a church in North Carolina where I was on staff. There were two middle-aged men in the church who passed away unexpectedly within the same year. They both attended the church regularly and both of them left family behind. The response to the two men's death seared the importance of prioritizing community into my mind forever.

The first man had invested deeply at the church. He served on a team. He encouraged his daughter to attend the student ministry. He participated in a small group Bible study. But more importantly, all of this represented his priority of building community into his life. The day he died, I arrived at his widow's home to the most beautiful, heart-rending sight. Her home was already full of people who had come to care for the family before any of the pastors had arrived. These friends supported his family for years after his death too. His priority of investing in and building community paid back a hundredfold in his family's time of need.

Contrast this with the second man who died. He attended church but didn't make building community a priority. He didn't serve, didn't participate in a group, and didn't encourage his kids to engage with the student ministry. His lack of formal participation exposed his lack of interest when it came to building community. The day he passed away, the people present at his home were the church's paid staff. We organized care for his family, which the church gladly participated in, but the difference in support was palpable.

I have never forgotten this visible, yet tragic, lesson in the importance of prioritizing community. You may not feel you need it today, but when you need it most, it may be too late.

HOW TO PRIORITIZE COMMUNITY

For most people "making it a priority" means saying to themselves in the back of their mind *I really should do more of that.* This, of course, changes nothing. As a mentor once told me, "Priorities are what you do, everything else is just talk." To unlock the power of priorities in your life and to apply this power to building community, you need to understand what priorities are.

Priorities are:

- what you schedule first
- what you schedule around
- what wins in a scheduling conflict

In other words, if you show me your calendar, I can tell you what your priorities are. There is no need for commentary. The practical application of this is that you need to put community building on your calendar. This is based on a proverb from the Bible about friendship:

"A man who has friends must be a friend,

but there is a friend who stays nearer than a brother" (Prov. 18:24 NLT).

If you want to have friends, you have to act friendly toward people. In other words, you have to be a community builder.

One obvious way to build community is to sign up for a small group or a serving team at your church. This will build the regular rhythm of community into your calendar. If you want to amplify this community building in your life, then set aside one hour or one half hour per week, perhaps your Wednesday lunchtime, to reach out to people you would like to build community with. Send them a text or an email if you aren't super close. Pray for them and let them know it. Ask them how you can pray for them. Ask them how life is going and listen. When community is scheduled in your calendar, you'll be amazed at how it grows.

The other way to be a community builder is to set aside money in your budget for these same people, even if it's only $20 a month. If you don't have a budget, just put a $20 bill in an envelope when you get paid and label it "For Friends." Then get creative. I've had a friend surprise me with a book and a cold-brew coffee delivered to my home. Heather and I once dropped toilet paper off at a friend's home during a thunderstorm because they ran out. We've given gift cards to friends for a date night. We've watched kids overnight so friends can escape on a mini-vacation. Years ago, one friend bought Heather a plant that we still have. Today that plant is pretty bedraggled, but we still think of our friend every time we see it. When community is in your budget, you'll be amazed at how it grows.

When you decide to connect, you are putting yourself in the environment where growth happens. You are a reflection of your five closest friends. So decide to connect and watch as God works to help you grow spiritually.

T he city isn't just for young people looking to advance in their careers nor is it mostly single-again people living near the action. Cities pick up everyone, and one of our most interesting families was the Rabens family.

Clay was an active-duty doctor for the Army. He found himself in the city because the military was sending him to Harvard School of Public Health. If you weren't aware that the Army sent people to Harvard, then welcome to the club.

When Clay walked in the door of our church, he came with his two amazing teenage daughters, Madison and Jocelyn. Those two girls were godly, mature, and hard workers. They grew our youth ministry from zero to two. If you're good at math you know that is infinity percent growth. By percentage, in my opinion, we were the fastest growing youth ministry in the universe.

Even more impressive than his daughters was his wife, Brittany. She was a force of nature who could organize and improve the second coming of Jesus. Her passion for Jesus was off the charts, and when you met her, you instantly liked her. Within a day, you knew she was probably a better leader than you. She was that good.

When you are a Harvard educated army doctor who is the fourth most impressive person in your family, that's really saying something.

What we learned from the Rabens family is the impact you can have when you decide to make a difference from day one. Because they were military, they already knew what so many in the city take too long to learn: if you've only got a year or two, then you need to invest from day one, otherwise you will miss out on the meaningful relationships or the impact you would have had.

The second week they came, the Rabens joined our church as members. A month later, Brittany was leading the outreach ministry to Mary Ellen McCormack, the largest, low-income housing development in the city. Within a few months, she was leading a small group with a mix of church attenders and housing development residents. By the end of the year, one of our friends from Mary Ellen McCormack was baptized in a repurposed horse trough in a one hundred-year-old high school because of Brittany's influence in her life.

It would have been so easy for the Rabens to coast for the one year they lived in Boston. There were good reasons to just wait and join a church when they moved away to Ohio, or they could have visited six other city churches before they made a decision on where to worship. Our church wasn't a great fit for them demographically. I mean, we didn't even have one other teenager. Yet Clay and Brittany learned something from the Army that can benefit every person who ever moves to a city: when time is limited "good enough" is good enough. Find a place where you can make an impact and throw yourself into it because you might change someone's eternity, like the Rabens did.

You have the same choice to make. You can wait for the "perfect" church, you can coast until you move somewhere more permanent, or you can decide to invest right now, right where you are, and make a difference. I'm not talking about going to a church that teaches heresy or not caring about doctrine. I'm talking about dialing down the "picky-meter" for the sake of making an impact.

BARRIERS TO SERVICE

Three of the most common barriers to serving in the city are the overwhelming need outside of the church, narcissism inside the church, and good old-fashioned scheduling.

One reason people don't jump in and make a difference at their church is because there is an overwhelming need for people to serve outside the church. Socially conscious companies have volunteer programs, boys and girls clubs need mentors, the Red Cross needs workers, and the city sponsors trash cleanup day. Those things are good, and we do all those things, but they are no substitute for loving God's people.

Another reason people don't serve in the city is a little embarrassing, but it's true. Narcissism is rampant in the city. Image matters, and people strive to be seen on social media as serving, but when it gets hard, people leave off from helping. We once had a person stop serving because they were asked to stop taking selfies while they were greeting guests. They were so offended they quit!

Narcissism used to be called vanity, which is excessive pride in one's appearance or accomplishments. You've never run into anyone like that in the city, have you? The real danger of vanity is that you are so busy looking in the mirror that you can't see yourself clearly. Jeremiah 4:30 (NIV) talks about the dynamics of narcissism:

"Why dress yourself in scarlet and put on jewels of gold? Why highlight your eyes with makeup? You adorn yourself in vain. Your lovers despise you."

The way narcissism works is that you spend all your money to look nice on the outside, to cover your insecurities on the inside, and to impress people that don't even like you.

However, the number one reason people don't get in the game right away and start making an impact is that they are overscheduled. In the suburbs, this tends to manifest through kids' sports, but in the city, it shows up in overscheduled social commitments, non-stop recreational activities, or an unhealthy rhythm of work and rest. Maybe you are overscheduling yourself because you don't know how to be alone with Jesus or with yourself. Maybe you can't stop working because your achievements are your life; they are how you justify your existence.

The beautiful thing about following Jesus is that He sets you free from all of this. Trusting in His wise leadership of the world lets you place your desperate needs at His feet. Trusting in His love for you can heal the wound that causes vanity to spring forth. Jesus justifies you with His blood so that you don't have to try to justify yourself with your accomplishments. Jesus once said, "my yoke is easy and my burden is light" (Matt. 11:30 NIV) and He meant it. When you follow Him, you can relax and slow down enough to care for and serve the people in your life. You can make a difference because of the difference Jesus has made in you.

YOU ARE NEEDED NOW

"If you were walking down the street and you saw a pinky finger lying on the ground what would your first thought be?" I always ask this question to people who live in Boston and the answers are hilarious and morbid (which reminds me of my family). I've heard everything from "The mafia is making a comeback" to "Seems about right." Now, if you haven't had your sense of humor twisted by the city, then you should answer, "That doesn't belong there." In the same way, when you see a brick laying by itself on the ground you realize, "That's not supposed to be lying there by itself. It's supposed to be a part of something bigger." In this metaphor, you are a severed pinky finger. You have a part to play in something bigger than yourself.

The Bible says that a church is like a body, and that Christians are like parts of that body.

"Now you are the body of Christ,
and each one of you is a part of it" (1 Cor. 12:27
NIV).

This means that if you are a Christian you are unique, you fit together with others, and you are needed right now. If the church is a body, it has no appendix. Every part is necessary. Let me say it again, you are needed now.

This is doubly true in the city because people are coming and going at a breathtaking rate. You are needed now because one third of your church left the city last spring. You are needed now because, if you are only here for two years, you can't afford to waste one. You are needed now because God is at work now, and you don't want to miss out on it.

THE BENEFIT OF SERVING

If you jump in to making a difference by serving others at a church right away, the impact will show up in your life in hugely positive ways. This is true if you are already a believer or if you are still exploring faith. You will build unforced relationships with other people because you have shared interests. You will become more selfless and less self-centered as you focus on others. And, perhaps best of all, you will learn and grow.

The Bible says that every person who puts their faith in Christ receives a spiritual gift. According to Pastor JD Greer, "A spiritual gift is usually just a special empowerment—an unusual effectiveness—in an assignment given to all believers."[3]

Like most gifts in the Bible, they aren't meant to be hoarded but shared. Think about it. When God blesses you with money, is it to hoard or share generously? When God gives you influence, is it to make you look good or to help others? Your spiritual gift from God is not something you should cling to, thanking God that you are a special snowflake. It is something to be used to help other people.

---

[3] *Gaining by Losing*, JD Greer, 2015, p. 144.

The way you discover your spiritual gift is not by taking tests online. Those things are fun, but they mostly reflect the gifts you wish you had. You discover your spiritual gifts by serving others and then watching for where God tends to work. One of the greatest benefits of serving is that you discover who God has uniquely made you to be and the spiritual gift He has given you.

GOD GOING PUBLIC

In his great book *The Beginner's Guide to Spiritual Gifts*, author Sam Storms says, "Spiritual gifts are the presence of the Spirit Himself coming to relatively clear, even dramatic, expression in the way we do ministry. Gifts are God going public among His people."

I love that definition. It's as though you realize, "Wow, God is really working here." The way God shows off through your life is when you get involved in serving others. It could be when you encourage someone you're serving with. It might be when you help someone figure out God's direction for his life. It could be hosting friends over to your home. Or it might be something more dramatic: prayers answered quickly, God-given insight into someone's situation, or something you feel God wants you to say to build someone up.

When those types of things happen, God is going public through you. And those things tend to happen when you are actively engaged in serving others.

WHEN YOU DECIDE TO MAKE AN IMPACT

When you decide to make an impact by serving others, it allows people to sense God in a real way in their life. Have you ever gone through periods of life when you didn't sense God in a way you could understand? That is happening to someone all the time.

When you serve because you follow Jesus (serving "in Jesus's name"), wonderful things occur:

- Lonely people experience God's presence through you.

- Exhausted people experience God's strength through you.

- Anxious people experience God's peace through you.
- Grieving people experience God's comfort through you.
- Confused people learn God's plan through you.

When you decide to make a difference by serving, God shows up in a way people can understand. He does it through you.

CHAPTER 5

DECIDE TO BE SINGLE WELL

O ne of the people I admire in Boston is a man named Altimesh. He is in his thirties and single, never married. He is quick with a loud laugh and a big smile. He's the kind of guy you would call to bail you out of jail at 3:00 a.m. because he is loyal to a fault. His knowledge of the Boston scene is unparalleled. He was the first friend to take me to Hawthorne's Bar in the basement of the Commonwealth Hotel, and, if you ever come to Boston, you must visit Hawthorne's.

Altimesh is Northern Indian by descent and grew up in Atlanta attending an Indian Orthodox church. If you don't know what an Indian Orthodox church is like, you are in good company. They sing the exact same songs fifty-two weeks per year. Every year. Forever. In Revelation, it says that people from every tribe, nation, and tongue will be singing songs of praise to the Lamb, and there will probably be an Indian Orthodox section where they just sing those same songs over and over and over again.

His family is traditional, and they want him to get married to a good Northern Indian girl. They want every interaction with the opposite sex to be in active pursuit of marriage. When his family calls, it's, "What's taking so long? What's the hold-up? Why aren't you married yet?" Actually, he has stopped answering the phone as frequently because of all the pressure.

One of the reasons Altimesh is a man I admire is because he does singleness well. He has come to measure singleness by God's Word. He has rooted himself in what Scripture says about marriage and singleness, but also what it *doesn't* say about it. He has come to embrace singleness as a way to love others, his community, and his city. I've watched as he leverages each moment of his life to give and serve others. I even watched as he volunteered to serve at a COVID field hospital in 2020, something it would be much more difficult for a married person to do.

He has, of course, struggled with feelings of missing out on marriage or feeling as though there is something he hasn't accomplished yet, but he has come to see singleness as a gift he wants to keep and embrace rather than one he wants to return. He does singleness well, and whether he is married or not, I admire the way he chooses to live.

SINGLE WELL

Some people feel called to singleness, but for most they are "single-for-now." It's likely that if you are single, you wish there was that special person in your life. You hope that marriage is in your future. However, if single is what you are, then it's important to do it well. Singleness is not a punishment, and it's not a means to an end. For most, singleness is a season, but whether for a long or short time, for all singleness is a gift. Let's explore what that means.

SINGLENESS IS A SEASON

A season is a period of life with a start date and an end date, but we don't usually know when the end date will be. The temptation of any season of life is to try to escape from it, to believe life will be better if we can end the season early. I see single people try to escape from singleness before their God-decided time, and it always ends poorly. Here are just some of the unhealthy ways people try to escape from singleness:

- giving their heart too quickly to a girlfriend or boyfriend
- getting into weirdly over dependent relationships with friends
- living together with a boyfriend or girlfriend
- compromising on who they marry

WARM AND WILLING OR HOT AND QUALIFIED?

By far, the number one way people try to escape their season of singleness is to compromise on whom they marry. Young Christians, in particular, compromise on who they choose because they are just so tired of being alone. If the person you are into has a lukewarm faith but they are around and into you, it can be tempting to go with the "bird in the hand." This can be disastrous.

Don't settle for warm and willing, wait for hot and qualified. Trust me on this one. Live by this simple rule and your future self will thank you. Wait for that person who has a red-hot, passionate pursuit of God and who matches the values and qualities you want in a spouse.

Proverbs is a book of the Bible that is a collection of sayings meant to transmit practical knowledge from one generation to the next. Proverbs are things that are true in most situations. Proverbs 31:10 says,

"A wife of noble character who can find?
She is worth far more than rubies" (Proverbs
31:10 NIV).

When you are looking for someone to marry, you are looking for someone who is more precious than rubies. This proverb also teaches us that a person with noble character will be hard to find. Don't miss this point. It's not supposed to be easy. You are looking for a needle in a haystack. You are searching for a diamond in the rough. Don't compromise on whom you marry to try to escape from a God-decided season of your life.

SINGLENESS AS A GIFT

Singleness is a gift, although you might wish that it came with a gift receipt. The gifts of God are almost always something to be shared, rarely something to be stockpiled. When God blesses you financially, the expectation is that you'll live generously. When God comforts you, He wants you to pay it forward and comfort those in distress. When God gives you forgiveness for your past, He wants you to be forgiving toward others. Singleness works the same way. God gives you singleness so that you can be a blessing to others with your time and energy.

When you are single, you can have a single-minded pursuit and devotion to serving Jesus:

An unmarried man can spend his time doing the Lord's work and thinking how to please him. But a married man has to think about his earthly responsibilities and how to please his wife. His interests are divided. In the same way, a woman who is no longer married or has never been married can be devoted to the Lord and holy in body and in spirit. But a married woman has to think about her earthly responsibilities and how to please her husband.

- 1 Corinthians 7:32-34 (NLT)

According to these sentences from Scripture, one of the greatest gifts of singleness is the ability to be solely focused in your pursuit of serving God. You don't have to spend the time, energy, and attention on a spouse that married people should be spending on one another.

While you have extra capacity and bandwidth to follow Jesus by serving people, it may be that you don't feel this way. You probably feel maxed out in your schedule and overwhelmed; you just need a break. You will probably feel this way until you get married and (hopefully) have children. When that day comes, you will say to yourself, "I had so much free time on my hands! Where has all my free time gone?"

If I am allowed to get real for a moment, in my experience with single people in the city I have often found they are incredibly busy with scheduled activities, but many of those activities are focused on themselves. Brunch with friends, a morning at the beach, hosting an out-of-town guest, a quick trip to a nearby city, and an evening with friends all make you feel busy, but they are activities focused on you. You have what you might call "disposable time" which, like disposable income, is time that you get to decide what to do with. Your disposable time is a gift.

Let me say it another way. Your downtime is a gift. The evenings when you don't have to put children to bed is a gift. Your ability to move and live wherever you want without consulting anyone is a gift. Your unilateral control over your schedule is a gift. Your ability to save money by living with roommates is a gift. Your full night of sleep without taking anyone else to the bathroom (unless you have a super weird relationship with your roommate) is a gift.

Remember, you get to decide whether those gifts are stockpiled and used for your enjoyment or passed on to others you can love and serve. Using your gifts to serve might look like babysitting for married couples. It might mean being the first one there to serve at church. It could mean surviving on ramen and dreams to attack your debt and also live an extravagantly generous life.

DIFFICULTIES

All this is not to say that singleness is easy.

It's not. *At all.*

It is to say that there are unique blessings in being single just like there are unique blessings in marriage. There are also unique challenges in singleness just like there are unique challenges in marriage. Singleness can be marked by a range of difficult emotions, less security, and a complicated relationship with sex.

You may feel you are missing out on the experiences or achievements of family life when you are single. In urban places, you will be surrounded by people who are young. Over time, they will go on to get engaged, get married, and have kids, and it's easy to feel as though you are missing out on something everyone else is experiencing.

In singleness, you are less secure. If you are married and one of you loses your job, you still have a remaining income to survive on. However, if you are single and lose your job, you could legitimately be living with your parents at the age of twenty-six. Being single, you might be plagued by feelings of being unwanted or not "marriage material," whatever that means. You might have to deal with incessant prodding from your parents (or entire extended family depending on your ethnicity and culture) to settle down and start a family.

And let's not forget that the Christian vision of singleness excludes sex with people you are not married to, so there's *that* whole issue which we don't even have space for in this book. Navigating sexuality while celibate is a skill set our culture does not prepare anyone for, but, suffice it to say, you can live without sex; you can't live without love.

There are blessings and there are challenges to singleness, but the question that shapes your time in the city is this: "What will I do with the gifts God has given me in my singleness?"

FINDING THE PURPOSE OF SINGLENESS

Singleness has its difficulties, but you can get through almost any "what" with a big enough "why." Do you know the "why" of your singleness? You must know the purpose of your singleness. I've heard it said that marriage shows the depth of God's love toward each individual person while singleness shows the breadth of God's love to the whole world.[4] I think there's a lot of truth to that. When you live singleness well, you get to show the world a picture of the God who has a single-minded devotion to loving and serving every person He has made.

Jesus was single, and this served to reinforce his single-minded devotion to do God's work in God's way. It also allowed Him to love widely and deeply without the constraints that marriage necessarily puts on affections. He modeled the purpose of singleness by living selflessly and sacrificially, giving His time, resources, and attention to love those around Him.

When you use the purpose of being single well, you help your friends, relatives, associates, and neighbors see God more clearly. When your singleness is self-focused, you show everyone a blurry picture of what God is like, but when your singleness is service-focused, you give people a crystal-clear picture of God's love.

---

[4] I heard Pastor Pete Scazzero say this at an Emotionally Healthy Marriage Conference in Queens, NY in 2018.

There is a purpose in your singleness. Fulfilling God's purpose for your singleness doesn't make it easier, but it makes it possible for you to get through. Purpose always gives you a reason to get through your difficulties.

A Note to Married People

Did you skip the last chapter because it was about singleness? Ha! Caught you red-handed! I know why you didn't read it; you escaped singleness, so good riddance. But I would like to encourage you to go back and read it for this simple reason: you will be surrounded by single people at church, and where you live and work. They will be asking you for advice because you're married. Instead of giving them platitudes and bumper stickers about singleness, why not absorb the last chapter so you can be a thoughtful and helpful friend? "You have to kiss a lot of toads before you find your prince" is usually true advice, especially when someone is using online dating apps, but I suspect you could do better. You could be a wise counselor for someone going through a difficult season of life. You will be glad you did.

CHAPTER 6
DECIDE TO LIVE GENEROUSLY

Adriana had been living and giving generously for years when God interrupted her plans. She quit her engineering job and moved far from her family because of her passion to help expose minority youth to the STEM fields. She was a capable engineer by anyone's standards, but the thing she cared about more than an engineering career was helping at-risk youth gain a larger vision for their lives; a vision that could be expanded by spending the summer at the Massachusetts Institute of Technology (MIT), visiting the Idea Lab, and watching people of color in action in the sciences.

Now, as many of you know, the only problem with following your passion is that passion doesn't pay the bills. Occasionally it does, but Adri had to take a 30 percent pay cut to take this job.

Adri soon discovered what so many people discover about moving to the city; it costs more—way more. Even if you make more, it's likely the money you make doesn't even begin to cover the increased costs. Adri had a decision to make: continue to live generously as she had for years or choose to delay generosity until another time in her life.

She chose generosity, and she will be the first to tell you that it doesn't make living in the city easier, but following Jesus is worth it. God has always taken care of her and provided what she needs, and, as a result, she can live generously without fear she will lack. Knowing this, she can continue the fight for educational justice for minority youth.

STELLA'S STORY

Another one of my favorite stories of generosity is from my friend Stella. She came to Boston from Mozambique via Nairobi and is wicked smart. She came to participate in a graduate program at Boston University and was accepted to the Sloan Management School at MIT. For Stella, money was beyond tight, but honoring her commitments to give generously came before everything.

One day, her car mysteriously disappeared, and I wanted to find out what happened. She told me, "I was expecting to get paid by my employer for the duration of my studies. As this didn't happen, the only way I could fulfill a vow I silently made to God [in Mozambique] was to sell my car. Which I did, and I gave 2/3 of the proceeds toward the building of a new church that will help reach out to more Mozambicans and lead them to salvation, like myself ten years ago."

She didn't have a car, but a few months after this decision, she had to go back home because of COVID. She no longer needed a car. God allowed her to be generous and made sure she never lacked.

These stories of generosity always make my heart beat faster because I know they represent ordinary people living by faith and following Jesus in an expensive, transient, secular place. I know because I've lived it too.

HOW MUCH MONEY I MAKE

I like to tell people how much money I make. A lack of transparency in this area has hurt a lot of people, made a few pastors very rich, and made a lot more pastors very poor. I feel it helps to address years of misconceptions and wondering. So let me tell you how much I make. I make between what a public schoolteacher makes and what a vice-principal makes. My wife works as a reading tutor and currently has three students, and she makes some money from that. My three kids don't make squat. Get a job, kiddos!

Why do I tell you about my income? First, I hope it sounds fair to you. My experience has been that pastors of city churches are paid comparably to the leaders of other non-profits of similar size in the city, usually less than the director of the local YMCA. Second, you need to know how much I make and how much my wife makes to appreciate what I'm about to tell you.

Heather and I have always tithed to the local church. Since we were teenagers, we've given 10 percent of our pre-tax earnings to God through whatever church we have attended. I tithe to the church I pastor, which is a little weird (why am I giving money back?), but the truth is, I want God's blessing on my finances, and I can't get that without giving to the Lord His due. However, last year, I felt God leading us to do more. We hadn't grown in generosity on a percentage basis, and we were getting comfortable.

We decided to increase our giving by 1 percent for the year, and if we could live like that, we would increase our giving by 1 percent the next year and keep doing so until we reached a point where we couldn't live anymore.

It was scary to step out in faith. What if the kids go to college but I don't have money saved? What if we don't have enough money to pursue that adoption we've been working on? What if there is a complete economic collapse due to a global pandemic in 2020 and we don't have enough saved? (Ok, we weren't worried about that, but we should have been.) In the end, we decided to choose faith and give, and you wouldn't believe what happened. The windows of heaven opened.

Multiple blessing showered us. We received part of an inheritance. When the coronavirus shutdown of 2020 happened, Heather's tutoring income doubled because kids weren't in school. We received a gift from a family member for no reason. We got our government stimulus checks. And on and on and on.

This year has been atypical. We've always given generously even in the years that I owed extra taxes, or my job cut everyone's pay 10 percent, or the time I started a small business and lost everything I invested. If you are having a tough year financially, you need God involved in your finances more than ever. The way to invite God to bless your finances is to give generously.

True faith often has a fear component you must overcome. That's why Jesus connected the dots between faith and fear for his followers:

*"He said to his disciples, 'Why are you so afraid?
Do you still have no faith?'" (Mark 4:40 NIV).*

True generosity requires you to believe that Jesus is greater than your worst fears. He is greater than your debts, your unemployment, and your bankruptcy. Jesus is even greater than your student loans. That's power.

According to the Bible, Jesus has a strange name for Himself that speaks to His power. I AM. It is a name for God from the Jewish Scriptures (the Old Testament) and it means something like "the eternally self-existing one." It means that Jesus has all the power and controls all the resources in the world.

It also means that your worst fears are no match for Jesus's power. To put it another way, your "What if?" is no match for His "I AM!"

GENEROSITY BARRIERS

It has been my observation that followers of Jesus want to be generous. This makes sense because

Jesus was generous with His money, His time, His attention, His power, and His life. Jesus didn't give a percentage of Himself for you. He gave every last ounce of Himself on the cross to inspire and enable you to live generously and to pay for your sin when you personally don't. God Himself is a generous God. The most famous verse in the Bible is about His generosity. It says that, "God so loved the world that he *gave...*" (John 3:16, emphasis mine). So it's no surprise that God's people long to be generous.

Whenever I am helping people diagnose why their generosity activity doesn't match their generosity desire, I run into the same handful of roadblocks every time.

GENEROSITY BLOCK #1 – A SCARCITY MINDSET

You long to be generous, but you may believe that you don't currently have enough to be generous. I call this a scarcity mindset. If you are having trouble making ends meet, it's natural to think, "I don't have enough to be generous like I want to be." There is also a version of this mindset that creeps in on wealthier friends (white-collar and up) who think, "I won't have enough in the future. I won't be able to fully fund my 401k or the 529 accounts for my kids' college, save for my next car, help my parents in retirement, and be generous like I want to be." It sounds insane if you are poorer, but trust me, people think like this all the time.

Instead of a scarcity mindset, whether rich or poor, God invites you to depend on His unlimited resources by giving generously. That's why Paul from Tarsus (aka the Apostle Paul) wrote:

"God is able to bless you abundantly, so that in all things at all times, having all that you need, you will abound in every good work... You will be enriched in every way so that you can be generous on every occasion" (2 Cor. 8-9:11 NIV).

When you give generously, you are stepping out in faith and inviting God into your finances. The word the Bible uses to describe how God blesses you is "abundantly." It says, "God is able" when you believe in His blessings by faith. You can live with an abundance mindset instead of a scarcity mindset. God will generously provide for you so that you can be even more generous. It's a virtuous cycle.

GENEROSITY BLOCK #2 – DEBT

Many Jesus followers long to be generous but are saddled with tens of thousands of dollars of debt. If you have not yet taken on student debt, we are begging you to stop and consider whether the career you are choosing will let you pay it back. We had a young woman at our church taking on $60,000 of debt per year to become a public-school teacher. Don't do it! But chances are good that if you are reading this book, you already have student loan debt of some kind, and you likely have consumer debt as well.

If that's you, then you can testify that the Bible is the completely TRUE Word of God because it says:

> *"The rich rule over the poor,*
> *and the borrower is slave to the lender" (Pro. 22:7*
> *NIV).*

When you are in debt, you don't control your own money anymore; your creditors have a claim to your paycheck every month before you decide what to do with it. You may desire to be generous, but your debt is holding you back from that.

If that's you, then you need to start being generous now and deal with your debt problem simultaneously. Go to Dave Ramsey's Financial Peace University, or a free community class, or whatever, but get your budget in order. [5] In Massachusetts, the average person will pay $261,220 of interest in their lifetime.[6] That means if you could completely avoid debt, you would be able to unleash that amount as generosity. It's a question of whether you're funding God's kingdom or Visa's kingdom.

---

[5] Go to www.DaveRamsey.com/fpu to get info or to sign up.

[6] Quentin Fottrell, "The Average American Pays $280,000 in Interest," MarketWatch (MarketWatch, January 14, 2015), https://www.marketwatch.com/story/the-average-american-pays-280000-in-interest-2015-01-14.

GENEROSITY BLOCK #3 – NO FINANCIAL SKILLS

Perhaps you want to be generous, but you don't know where your money is going. You don't have any financial skills.

Consider this scenario. Each evening you drink a glass of chardonnay and go on an internet clicking spree, buying junk you don't need and maybe won't even open to impress people you don't even like. You have no idea how much you spend eating out all the time. You eat on the go at lunch and order takeout for dinner. You have zombie charges from gyms you no longer attend and subscriptions you don't use. If Suze Orman were to see how much you spent on coffee last year, she would spontaneously burst into uncontrollable sobs. If you recognize any of this in yourself, you have a problem with your spending and your lack of financial skills.

I want you to know that being in this situation is okay. God loves you. I still love you. Jesus forgives you. You need to grow, however. Here is advice from the Bible from some sheep herders who had a better grasp of financial skills than most Americans:

"Be sure you know the condition of your flocks, give careful attention to your herds" (Prov. 27:23 NIV).

You need to develop the skills that will allow you to release unbelievable amounts of generosity in your lifetime. Again, the content is out there. Whether it's the Financial Peace University mentioned above or a community event you find on your own, you need financial skills to follow Jesus in generosity.

WHEN DESIRE DRAGS

Whenever I help people with generosity in the city, my default assumption is that they desire to be generous but something is holding them back. However, I have learned this is not always the case. Sometimes you just don't have the desire to be generous. The Bible would slap a label on this and call it greed. That seems pretty harsh to us, but if you get to the place in life where you are more focused on accumulation than generosity, what else would you call it?

When you are trying to get something from money that you can only get from God, you are on the pathway of greed. There are signs along this road:

- You want money to guarantee your security for the future.
- You want money to tell you that you're successful.
- You want money to help you feel accepted.
- You want money to live in perfect comfort.
- You want money to prove to your parents that you are not a failure.

When your net-worth determines your self-worth, you will never be truly generous. Why? Because you so desperately need money to shore up your identity. When your sense of security, success, acceptance, and comfort come from how much God loves you through Jesus, then money is just money. When money is just money, you are free to give it away generously. In Jesus there is freedom.

"Then you will know the truth,
and the truth will set you free" (John 8:32 NIV).

When you understand your self-worth and your net-worth are not the same thing, you are free to live generously.

IDEAS FOR EVERYDAY GENEROSITY

Once you are free to be generous, here are some useful ideas we have practiced and lived in the Kirk home.

SET A GIVING GOAL

I'm a goal-oriented person, so when I encountered this idea years ago,[7] I immediately set a goal to give away $100,000 in a single year even though my income was less than half that amount at the time. In 2019, my family started the process of international adoption out of our concern for orphans around the world. This was born out of a verse in the Bible which says,

> *"Religion that God our Father accepts as pure and faultless is this: to look after orphans and widows in their distress and to keep oneself from being polluted by the world" (James 1:27 NIV).*

---

[7] From the book *The Circle Maker* by Mark Batterson

At the end of the year paying for the adoption, we had spent thousands of additional dollars on fees to various agencies and governments. I was concerned about our family's bottom line until I realized we were making serious progress on our giving goals.

SET UP A FUND FOR MEETING PRACTICAL NEEDS

Have you ever noticed someone in your church or at the office going through a hard time financially and thought, "*I wish I could help, but things are tight for me.*" Consider setting aside any amount of money (even $5 to start) in an envelope every time you get paid. That money is now for meeting the needs of people having tough times. When you've got money set aside for it, you'll start to notice whom it will best serve. Giving anonymously and generously can be seriously fun.

START GIVING AUTOMATICALLY

When I go to the gym, I don't decide whether to pay each month depending on whether I feel like being in shape. I give them my credit card, and they take out the money automatically because I value my health. In the same way, when you decide to value generosity, set it up intentionally and automatically whenever you get paid. Many Jesus followers give to the church automatically when they receive their paycheck. Other people sponsor children in poverty around the world by setting up automatic payments on their credit card. I had a friend who, every time he got paid, automatically transferred 1 percent of his pay into a different checking account to meet any needs he encountered. You'll be surprised by just how generous you can be.

KEEP GIFTS IN YOUR CAR FOR THE HOMELESS OR ADDICTED

One of the toughest questions Christians ask who are new to the city is what to do about the homeless or people with addictions asking for money. First, let me say that you should follow your conscience. If you decide differently than me, I respect that. Second, let me tell you what the Kirk family does. We don't give money to people asking on the street. If we want to give financially, we give through well-known organizations dedicated to ending homelessness or addiction. Instead, we keep food in our car and offer that. We keep Ziplock bags with granola bars and toiletries for people who ask. That way it keeps our souls soft and we practice generosity to those struggling without directly and obviously helping them to buy drugs.

WORTH IT

When you talk to Adri or Stella from the beginning of this chapter, or millions of other Christians, you can ask any one of them whether generosity in the city is worth it. They will all tell you the same thing. If you are following Jesus, then you can follow Him anywhere, even into the city, and live His way. He will provide for you and that will grow your faith. The greatest blessing of all is that you will know Him more and depend on Him more. And knowing Jesus more is everything. He is worth it.

CHAPTER 7
DECIDE TO BE AN INFLUENCER

Meg was out for drinks with a co-worker after a particularly tough day teaching in the classroom. At first, the conversation was the usual stuff: asking each other for advice with challenging kids, wondering what on earth the administration is thinking, laughing about the crazy and amazing things teenagers say. But then the conversation took an unexpected, yet totally honest, turn.

Meg worked in one of the worst schools in the city. It was common in every class period that she taught to be interrupted by a behavioral issue. It wasn't the kids that made the school bad, although some kids in Boston can be tough to handle. It was the complete lack of support and the lack of a systematic discipline plan from the school administration. Teachers were quitting mid-year, parents were upset, and Meg was having trouble holding it together in her very first year of teaching.

Meg is one of many teachers in our church who follow Jesus into tough schools because she believes that every kid deserves a quality education. For many of these teachers, the racial component of educational disparity is part of what drives them. You can't have Jesus without justice, and these teachers live that out every day in the trenches. For these teachers, Black Lives Matter is neither a slogan nor an organization. It is a truth they pursue with their career as they follow Jesus to declare the value of each person by providing them with the education they need to thrive.

So Meg is sitting at a bar having drinks with a co-worker when the conversation gets personal. Her friend asks, "How are you getting through this? You are so strong!" Meg's answer hands down is one of my all-time favorite faith answers. It's simple, direct, and honest.

"I'm not strong!" she insists. "I have God in my life and God is strong. He gets me through it."

Meg relayed this story to me several weeks afterwards and it dawned on me that her answer mirrored a quote from the Bible. One of the greatest faith influencers of all time was Paul from Tarsus, and when he was talking about his ministry he made this claim:

"I will boast all the more gladly about my weaknesses, so that Christ's power may rest on me. That is why, for Christ's sake, I delight in weaknesses, in insults, in hardships, in persecutions, in difficulties. For when I am weak, then I am strong" (1 Cor. 12:9-10 NIV)

For Paul, weakness is the place where God's strength stands out. Darkness is where light appears brightest. Foolishness is where wisdom appears most clearly. Confusion is where conviction surprises most.

Meg took a huge step that day. She made the choice to leverage her influence to help a friend see how amazing God is.

INFLUENCERS

Let me share a statistic with you that will blow your mind *and* make you seriously consider whether college was a good investment or whether you should have stayed home filming yourself and uploading it to the internet.

Way back in 2018, Vox conducted an interview with the head of a talent agency that signs internet influencers to sell products and push brands. According to the article, an influencer is someone "with a strong relationship to an audience who can heavily sway decisions." [8] Now for the crazy part, listen to what the agency head had to say:

> A micro-influencer, which is someone that has 10,000 to 50,000 followers, is actually pretty valuable. They used to only pick up a couple

---

[8] Chavie Lieber, "How and Why Do Influencers Make so Much Money? The Head of an Influencer Agency Explains.," Vox (Vox, November 28, 2018), https://www.vox.com/the-goods/2018/11/28/18116875/influencer-marketing-social-media-engagement-instagram-youtube.

hundred bucks, but today, they get a minimum of a few thousand dollars a post.

Influencers with up to 1 million followers can get $10,000 per post, depending on the platform, and 1 million followers and up, you're getting into territory where they can charge $100,000. Some can even get $250,000 for a post! Especially if the content is on YouTube and the influencer is in the gaming industry.

An influential relationship with the audience is so valuable on Madison Avenue that they are willing to pay someone a quarter million dollars for a single post pushing their product. And that was in 2018, so what is it today?

Why do I bring this up? Because it shows your influence in other people's lives is valuable. It is the most precious thing you possess, and not because you can get people to buy things, but because you can influence your friends, associates, relatives, and neighbors in an eternal way. That is what Meg did when she boldly shared with her friend what was getting her through tough times.

INFLUENCE INGREDIENTS

When you become a faith influencer in the lives of others you are following in the footsteps of Jesus, whom I would argue is the greatest influencer of all time. He was utterly compelling in His personality, unmatched in His accomplishments, and unparalleled in His development of people. He built no organization, possessed no wealth, had no connections to powerful people, and still two billion people on earth look to Him as the leader of their lives.

From Jesus we can learn the ingredients of influence. These ingredients are who you must *be* in order to be an influencer in your circles. Relationship, boldness, and integrity are the key ingredients of influence. These ingredients are about who you are. They are principles proven to work. You get to choose whether you use them for a higher purpose.

RELATIONSHIP

Jesus operated with varying levels of relationships. He had three closest followers, twelve disciples (students), and about seventy followers. There were crowds that followed Him, but He didn't change the world through crowds; He changed the world through the Twelve. "His concern was not with programs to reach the multitudes, but with men whom the multitudes would follow."[9]

You already have networks of relationships with people built on mutual trust. You can add and strengthen these relationships by setting aside time in your calendar and money in your budget to do nice things for people. Now, many people worry about risking their relationships by bringing up faith, but what kind of relationships do you have if you can't speak about one of the most important things in your life?

BOLDNESS

Jesus was crazy bold with His message. He wasn't afraid to offend sensibilities or speak truth to those in power. He once let a lady cry on His feet at a

---

[9] Robert E. Coleman, *The Master Plan of Evangelism*

dinner party to make a point about how power and religion can dehumanize people. His absolute conviction behind what He said made people wonder if their assumptions about the world might be wrong. His depth of conviction pushed complacent people off-balance. Conviction is stunning in the midst of confusion.

You gain influence when you are bold with your faith. In my city, *everyone* is bold about their opinion. People don't hesitate to tell you what they really think about politics, or race, or what they had for breakfast. It was my friend Abby Dunn who pointed out one day, "No one I ever talk to in this city keeps their opinions to themselves. Why do I ever feel nervous about talking boldly about my opinions about faith? That's what everyone else is doing. That's what I'm going to do!" I have loved that statement ever since.

When you are bold with your faith, when you speak with depth of conviction, when you are passionate and excited by faith, you become a faith influencer in your friends' lives.

INTEGRITY

Jesus was the ultimate example of integrity. He was the one human whose life perfectly matched His message. The closer you got to Jesus, the better His life looked. He wasn't just a public figure. He was a man without sin. I've often wondered if this was why His mother and His brother, James, believed He was the sinless Son of God. They lived with Him, and they knew it was true.

When you lack integrity, it destroys your influence. My wife followed a lady on Instagram who was a self-styled "adoption influencer." She had a large family of adopted kids and a larger following because of that. Then, one day, someone noticed one of her adopted children had disappeared from all the pictures. She had moved this child out of her family but hadn't told anyone about it. It was just like those old Soviet photographs where people are "disappeared" for criticizing the regime. When her actions came to light, her influence evaporated. Integrity can't be faked forever. When you lack it, you lose influence.

INFLUENCING WHILE GROWING INFLUENCE

Influencing others in regard to faith is difficult. The dynamic at play is that the deeper the relationship you have with a person, the more you are risking the influence you've worked so hard to build. This is why it can be so hard to talk about faith with family and people in whom you have invested in the most. (Trust me, I know.) You are risking the influence you have worked so hard to earn.

However, you can influence others toward faith while simultaneously growing your influence with them. There are three actions that lead to this outcome.

PERMISSION

Have you ever brought up faith with someone and they looked profoundly uncomfortable? In the early days of my faith, I did this all the time with my family. Faith in Jesus had made such an amazing difference in my life that I assumed it would be natural and welcome in conversations with my family. Boy, was I wrong! It's not because they are closed-off people; they are not. It was because I lacked tact and I violated the law of permission.

If you are going to talk about faith with people who don't normally talk about it, then you need to create safety for them in the conversation. The way you do this is simple: give them permission to say "no" by asking their permission to talk about it.

If they say "no," don't sweat it. Why talk to someone who doesn't want to talk to you? But every person I've ever asked has said, "yes." Every one. That's because when you have permission you can say anything and it's safe for them.

CURIOSITY

I once shared about how Jesus changed my life with a Zoroastrian at a kid's birthday party. That is a weird sentence, but it is nowhere as weird as that birthday party. I shared a little about the story earlier, but you still may wonder how did this conversation come about?

In fairness, I'm a second-rate evangelist, but I found myself in this position because I was so unbelievably fascinated by this person's religion that I asked dozens of questions. Eventually, she asked what I believed and why my belief was captivating to me, so I got to tell her about just how amazing Jesus is. Curiosity opens the door to dialogue.

People may perceive Christians as judgmental, but curiosity is the antidote to that. When you don't understand why people do what they do, start asking to learn in a gracious way. Of all the questions Jesus was asked, He only gave a direct answer to three of them. Most of the time, He answered with another question. Be curious; you never know what doors your curiosity will open.

People are endlessly fascinating. Your questions can open the doors to personal stories, opinions about the church, and views on God. So be curious.

GENEROSITY

The more generously you live, the more influence you will have. My first youth pastor, Garland Robertson, modeled this for me early on in my faith. He has the spiritual gift of giving. When he went on a trip, he would come back with some little trinket for you. When you went out to eat, he picked up every check. He paid for Miami Hurricanes football games and movies. Everything he did involved generosity, and as a result, people wanted to be around him. Generosity grew his influence.

Generosity of time, generosity of gifts, generosity of attention, and generosity of promoting other people's projects all open the doors to influence others. This is how people closed to you become open people. It's how their perception of Christians changes and how they can begin to consider your faith. It's how you earn the right to speak in someone else's life.

INFLUENCE IN THE CITY

As with everything else in life, the city adds a layer of complexity to following Jesus. In previous chapters, I've touched on the challenge of the loss of cultural capital. When it comes to influencing others toward faith, this is experienced as a host of negative perceptions about Christians. We can add to the list of challenges a preponderance of scientific careers, a disproportionate number of people trained by secular/progressive learning institutions, a lack of disposable time and income, and much more. You can easily fixate on the negatives and bum yourself out.

However, the city provides unique opportunities when it comes to deciding to be a faith influencer. Cities are disproportionately young. Cities begin to deconstruct an unexamined or incoherent worldview almost as soon as a person arrives. Cities are filled with people who have lost their attachments to tradition. And lastly, cities are a place of inquisitiveness and openness to new ideas. All of these are God-decided opportunities to influence your friends, relatives, associates, and neighbors toward faith.

When your life matches your words and your words are bold, it is a powerful statement others can't ignore. When your relationships are fueled by curiosity, generosity, and safety, God will do incredible things through you. Just like Meg, whom we talked about at the beginning of this chapter, the goal is not to be strong. The goal is to be real. Your weakness in leaning on God to help you in the city is where His power shines brightest. That's the kind of faith influence our cities need.

CHAPTER 8
DECIDE TO PURSUE UNITY

In liberal and progressive circles, there is language around being "woke," which in example is to say something like, "Have you woken up to see that conservatives are complicit in racism and that racial disparities are a result of systems, structures, and policies designed to create precisely this result?" The implication of being "woke" is that you've had an awakening and you now see it everywhere. Being "woke" is common parlance (at least as this book is written).

Did you know that conservatives have a similar saying? They call it getting "red-pilled," and it is stereotypically conservative that their slogan isn't as catchy or as cool as the progressive one. It references an old movie called *The Matrix* when the protagonist takes a red pill and wakes up to discover he was living in a dream. The implication is something like, "Have you had an awakening to see that progressives have lost all touch with reality and that individual choices are what most profoundly shapes your life regardless of racial identity?" The implication of getting "red-pilled" is that you've had an awakening and now you see it everywhere.

Isn't it interesting that in American society, which is undoubtedly racialized, groups of people have created language to describe an awakening to a whole new way of understanding the world, especially in regard to race?

Christians have a way of talking about an awakening that changes the way you view race and ethnicity (along with everything else). We call it being "born again" and it comes straight from Jesus.

"Very truly I tell you, no one can see the kingdom of God unless they are born again" (John 3:3 NIV).

Jesus used the language of being born again because in that day and time almost everything about your identity was determined by your birth. Your ethnicity, your religion, your occupation, your economic status—everything about you—was determined by your natural birth. However, according to Jesus, if you want to perceive the kingdom of God in this world, (to have an awakening to where you see it everywhere) you need to be born again.

Then, your fundamental identity no longer comes from the blood in your veins, but the blood in His veins. Your perception of your neighbors and your world comes from your adoption into God's family. When this fundamental identity shift happens, you start to see God's kingdom advancing everywhere, and that shapes your views of race and ethnicity.

If your faith doesn't affect your perception of race in America, then your identity as an American is more fundamental than your identity as a follower of Jesus.

Because you live in the city, you will quickly be confronted by the reality of whether or not you have ever grappled with issues of race and multiculturalism.

YOU MUST GROW

When you live in the city, it's not surprising that your cultural awareness needs to rise if you are going to live and work with people from very different backgrounds than yourself. Yet, have you ever considered that your cultural awareness is going to have to grow for you to worship in the city?

The earliest church struggled with issues of unity because the stratified and divided Roman society of the first century was reflected in the early church. Dealing with ethnic division is one of the primary issues the early church faced, but a great many Christians are unaware that such things are even addressed in the Scriptures. Call it a "blind-spot" if you are charitable. Call it an "error" if you are honest. Some believe it to be "willful ignorance," but whatever it is, you need your theology updated to live in unity in the midst of diversity.

THE GOAL IS NOT DIVERSITY

The first thing you will notice reading the letters the earliest Christian leaders wrote (collected together as the New Testament) is that diversity is not a goal in and of itself. There were major struggles about whether to diversify the early church, and then concerning what kind of role and rules applied to the new ethnic groups joining to follow Christ.

The goal for the early church was not diversity *per se*, but rather, building unity among diverse people. Your corporation might want diversity, and that's a good thing, but the church's goal is to build unity among diverse people, and that's a much harder thing. The early church leaders gained this emphasis on unity from Jesus who said,

> *"Holy Father, protect them by the power of your name, the name you gave me, so that they may be one as we are one" (John 17:11 NIV).*

Whenever you find language of "unity," "love," or "Jews" and "gentiles" in the Bible, you are in the thought world of diverse ethnicities learning to live together.

Here are a few of the examples you may never have noticed before if you grew up in predominantly white evangelical churches, or you may not know about these if you are new to the Bible. The list isn't exhaustive, but it serves to show you how prevalent this concept is in the Bible.

PREDICTIONS ABOUT ETHNIC UNITY

In the Old Testament (which are the Jewish Scriptures), the idea shows up repeatedly that God is going to one day unify diverse people, bringing peace and justice to the world, by drawing all people to Himself. Here is my favorite example:

"It is too small a thing for you to be my servant to restore the tribes of Jacob and bring back those of Israel I have kept. I will also make you a light for the Gentiles, that my salvation may reach to the ends of the earth" (Isa. 49:6 NIV).

PENTECOST IS ABOUT ETHNIC UNITY

At Pentecost, the Holy Spirit came upon people for the first time and they started proclaiming how amazing God is in all the languages of the world.[10] This is clearly the undoing of the tower of Babel

---

[10] Acts 2:1-13

incident when languages were scattered and ethnic conflict was born.[11] Pentecost is a sign that God is healing division.

DEACONS CREATED TO DEAL WITH AN UNJUST SYSTEM

When the church was an infant, it distributed food to its widows, but the Greek widows were being discriminated against in favor of the Jewish widows. This was an injustice based on ethnicity that showed up in the food distribution system. Deacons were appointed to fix the inequity.

ETHNIC SEGREGATION CALLED OUT

When Peter travelled to Antioch, he originally ate with the Gentiles, even though he was a Jew, as a sign of their inclusion in the family of Jesus. However, when Jews arrived from Jerusalem, Peter reverted to self-segregation to maintain a sense of

---

[11] Genesis 11:1-8

racial purity. The apostle Paul calls him out for not "acting in line with the truth of the gospel" (Gal. 2:14 NIV).

THEOLOGICAL TEACHING ON ETHNIC DIVISION

More than a few places in the New Testament reference the idea that, in relation to God, ethnic barriers have been eliminated; therefore within God's family, those barriers ought not divide. Here's an example:

"There is neither Jew nor Gentile, neither slave nor free, nor is there male and female, for you are all one in Christ Jesus" (Gal. 3:28 NIV).

ALL THIS TO SAY...

I point out all of these examples to raise your consciousness that the Bible has both the language and resources to address ethnic and racial tensions and to build unity among diverse peoples. When the Bible talks about the way of unity, it uses words like "love," "justice," and "humility." One of my favorite passages that teaches the way forward for racial unity in the local church is this:

> *"Do nothing out of selfish ambition or vain conceit. Rather, in humility value others above yourselves" (Phil. 2:3 NIV).*

It doesn't sound like contemporary language around racial awareness or cultural competency, but the advice (command if you are a follower of Jesus) is still good. It works because it's based on God's wisdom and the way He made people.

NEITHER/NOR

Here's the funny thing. Conservatives always assume that I'm a liberal for caring about unity in the local church and acknowledging that it has a strong racial component. Liberals assume that I'm a conservative because of my views on human sexuality.

If you are a Christian, I believe it to be an error to slide neatly into an ideology constructed by political commentators. Christians don't follow an ideology, we follow Jesus. Those who don't know the Lord might label you in an attempt to fit you into their ideology. However, we aren't defined by labels, we are defined by following our Savior.

WORK TO DO

You've got a role to play when it comes to building unity from diversity in your church. It's one thing to have a community committed to racial unity, but it's something different to be engaged in this pursuit yourself.

From living in the city, we've learned some things you need to be aware of and some things you need to actively do in order to be a unity builder wherever God has you.

EDUCATION

The first thing you can do is educate yourself about multicultural churches and race in America. This is so common to say that it's almost a cliché, but it's no less true. The danger, of course, is that all such works are polemical, and may or may not have a scriptural basis.

The simplest thing you could do would be to ask your pastor which books to read on the subject. At Renewal, I recommend people read both non-fiction and more literary works such as *Divided by Faith* by M.O. Emerson or *Narrative of the Life of Frederick Douglass* by Frederick Douglas.

FRIENDSHIP

You'll never be a unity builder in your church if you don't have a multi-cultural life. The diversity of perspective in your circle of friends should broaden and enrich your view of everything God has done for you in Christ.

Inviting people into your home or visiting them in theirs is the quickest way to move the relationship from an acquaintance to a friend. Roommates and cramped spaces can make this tough in a city, but there are ways to make it work. Have them meet up at your place before you go somewhere. Eat ramen and watch a show with your roommates around; it's not the end of the world.

SEEK PERSPECTIVE

Your church may look ethnically diverse but feel culturally monolithic to minorities who attend. If your church's membership is under 30 percent minority, it is highly likely that it has a predominant culture that is normative to a specific ethnicity (a "black" church, a "white evangelical" church, a "Korean Presbyterian" church, etc.). This means that people who are in your church's minority experience worship, church structure, and spiritual authority in very different ways than you do.

When you seek other's perspective, you invite honest dialogue about how people from other ethnicities see the world and your church. Avoid asking them to speak in generalities about their ethnicity or race and instead ask for their unique perspective. Your curiosity will keep your judgementalism at bay, and you'll be living out some of the greatest advice in the whole Bible:

"Everyone should be quick to listen, slow to speak, and slow to become angry" (James 1:19 NIV).

WORK THAT MATTERS

I've written from an American perspective, but the sin of partiality is a temptation for every human heart. The simple truth is that when our churches are divided ethnically, we are mirroring the division of our wider societies. We are losing our witness that Christ can do something new and different in people.

However, when the church is actively building unity out of diversity, we give the world a taste of something distinct, and our unity shows the power of God to make us human again. You can decide to be a unity builder and increase the fame of Jesus in your city. It is in your power.

I was seven hours into the loudest fourteen-hour drive of my life due to cardboard duct-taped onto the window of my car. We were headed to North Carolina's Outer Banks for our annual family vacation, and we had instituted a shoes-stay-on order with the children because of all the shards of glass on the floorboard. I was seriously considering whether I wanted to go back and live in the city when my vacation was over.

The Wednesday before, my community group gathered in my home. They were a motley crew, but they were my crew: a man who grew up in a Korean house church who now had some serious issues with authority; a woman well under twenty-five, whose husband had recently left her, was exploring a faith she would eventually walk away from; a nutty (yet charming in his way) professor and his archivist wife; and a young idealist using her talents in working with youth at the local YMCA.

We were packing twenty shoeboxes for Operation Christmas Child. When we were done, our home had twenty giftwrapped shoeboxes filled with toothbrushes, socks, pencils, toys, and a little bit of hope in Jesus's name for kids all over the world. On Saturday night before church, I decided to try something new and actually be a helpful husband. I carried the boxes to the car so that Heather wouldn't have to carry them out in the morning.

When I woke up on Sunday morning, I went to get my Bible from the car before I left for this day's services, but before I could open the car door, I knew what had happened. Someone had busted out our window and stolen the gifts intended for twenty less fortunate kids.

Today I think it's hilarious to imagine a likely homeless drug addict opening dozens of boxes of what he thought were the latest Yeezy's, only to discover instead exactly what he needed to live:

toothbrushes, socks, pencils, and some bonus toys to fight the boredom of not having a job. But at the time, I was not laughing. I was *mad.* And to top it off, I had to drive fourteen hours to my vacation that afternoon.

CENTRIFUGAL FORCE

It's not just petty crime that makes you question whether you should stay in the city long-term. It's everything. The city has a centrifugal force that expels you outward. For all but the wealthiest people, the costs, crime, and concerns of city living tend to push you toward the suburbs.

The cost of city living pushes you outward. It's well known among Bostonians that cost-of-living adjustments cannot begin to make-up for the cost differential of housing. I was once on a trip outside of Charlotte, North Carolina when I was unexpectedly offered a job there. I had no sense of calling to the place or any sense that God had released me from His work in Boston, but that night I looked up local homes on the internet. I found a historic five-bedroom house in a lakefront community for $100,000 less than my condo in Roxbury. It was an instantaneous temptation to skip asking God what He wanted me to do and settle for quick comfort outside of God's will. A friend later warned me that real estate websites are like pornography for city-dwellers, and I promptly killed that habit.

The crime you experience in the city pushes you outward as well. Including the theft of presents for disadvantaged kids, I had my car broken into three times in a two-year span. A young family in the church came to our neighborhood to explore whether they should live near us. When they arrived at our house, the police had a suspect face down on my next-door neighbor's driveway and there were thirty more officers with dogs searching for his gun. The police found the gun and the young family found another neighborhood to live in.

In addition, the growing concerns of schooling, adequate housing for children, and lack of long-term relationships will push you out from the city. With kids, you immediately start thinking about schooling. If you live in a major city, good luck at finding the perfect place. There are some hidden gems, but those schools are tough to get into. Then, what if you want to have a larger family? The cost of an extra bedroom makes the cost of having another child astronomical.

With all of these concerns, you may wonder why anyone would choose to stay in the city long-term or even longer-term. There are plenty of reasons to move out of the city as soon as you have gotten from it what you want, but there are good and godly reasons to stay or at least to extend your season in the city.

CENTRIPETAL FORCE

There is an energy to the city that comes from the tension of different types of people crammed into the same space. Cities are the stomping grounds of creatives and entrepreneurs. Universities anchor and enrich the intellectual landscape of cities.

For me personally, there are two things that anchor me in the city. The first is a sense that God has asked me to be here to equip urban professionals to impact global cities for Christ. That sense of God's direction has held me fast when things get difficult. The second thing that anchors me are my neighbors on Thwing Street. I live on the weirdest street in Boston. It is as diverse as Sesame Street with 100 percent less puppets.

On Thwing Street lives a retired ballet dancer with a penchant for original outfits and her French artist husband. A few doors down, a woman I deeply respect has been here for a generation. Her ex-husband invites me on Peace Walks with Twelfth Baptist Church. Our neighbors on one side are an anesthesiologist and a pharmacist. My other neighbor is an elderly woman who is super sweet, but her house legitimately looks like it's haunted. There is the interesting couple who just seems to work together; she is Indian and he is Jewish, so the Lord only knows what their mothers thought of their marriage. Down from them lives a school-teacher beer-brewer who runs marathons at the age of forty and is always working in the yard shirtless, possibly just to prove he is in better shape than me. All of the kids ride bikes on Thwing Street together, and as unique and one-in-a-million as all these people are, I know they see the "minister" down the street (that's what they call me) as an oddity and, hopefully, an addition.

These are talented, quirky, kind people who I wish had the type of relationship with God that is life-giving, marriage-saving, and eternity-shaping. They aren't moving to the suburbs because the suburbs are too boring to contain people like them. And I don't want to leave them.

IN THE CITY FOR THE CITY

When Jesus talked about His followers' role in society, He made a very famous statement about light. Maybe you've heard it:

> *You are the light of the world—like a city on a hilltop that cannot be hidden. No one lights a lamp and then puts it under a basket. Instead, a lamp is placed on a stand, where it gives light to everyone in the house. In the same way, let your good deeds shine out for all to see, so that everyone will praise your heavenly Father.*
> - Matthew 6:14-16 NLT

Jesus's followers are like a city inside the city. They live different lives full of healthy relationships, generosity, selflessness, service, and worship. Because their lives are different, they shine like light in the darkness. As a city within a city, they show the way forward for the wider cities in which we live. Followers of Jesus are in the city for the city.

Unlike the other decisions in this book, which I hope everyone will make, I don't expect everyone to stay in the city long-term. You must follow God's plan for your life, but be careful if God's plan sounds like a bigger house and an easier life. Your decision must be how to love the city God has placed you in for this season rather than using the vitality of the urban environment for your own ends.

POSSIBILITIES

Loving your city for a longer period than you thought is not an all-or-nothing proposition. There are possibilities for how you can make an ongoing kingdom impact. These possibilities include choosing to live in the center-city, staying for longer, and paying it forward.

You can choose to locate in the city on purpose. Instead of commuting in from the suburbs for work, choose to live and worship in the city. You'll trade living space for urban impact, and you'll gain back commuting time and lower your carbon footprint.

You could stay for longer. Many urban professionals I speak with are planning on staying in the city for "a couple years." In reality, this means they are here until they can get promoted or land a better job. What you might not see is how your contribution to Jesus's work in the city could be multiplied by staying an extra year or two. Most of the urban churches I work with consider a married couple who stays for five years a pillar of the church. A person who commits another year or two is like oxygen to a local church. Staying for longer will also give you the time you need to invest in relationships that God may use to help other people find faith.

Of course, you may not be able to stay in the city because of your school schedule or your career track. However, you might be able to pay it forward. Every single year, people in our church decide to give financially to support the church after they leave. Why? Because they want to make a way for the next generation of urban professionals to experience the life-changing environment of a vibrant church just like they did. Deciding to give a monthly gift in any amount to a church you leave is an investment in God's work in the city.

Lastly, you can decide to stay. As you pray about this, you may feel God leading you to stay in the city long-term. There are significant costs to following the leading of God (more than monetary), but I always come back to this verse:

"Truly I tell you," Jesus replied, "no one who has left home or brothers or sisters or mother or father or children or fields for me and the gospel will fail to receive a hundred times as much in this present age: homes, brothers, sisters, mothers, children and fields—along with persecutions—and in the age to come eternal life"
(Mark 10:29-30 NIV).

When you decide to stay in the city long term, there are costs associated with that, but there are also benefits. I don't mean the amenities the city offers. I mean the spiritual family Mark 10:29-30 talks about as well as how the difficulties press you into God and invite His glory in to fill your life. There is a cost to following Jesus, whether He leads you back to the town you grew up in to reach your family and friends or whether He leads you to stay in the city. Yet isn't that the true adventure of following Jesus? You never know where He will lead you.

WHAT I WANT FOR YOU

Ultimately, what I want for you is not to stay in the city long-term. I want you to follow Jesus wherever He leads you. I want you to chase His presence and His power more than you chase your next promotion. I want you to come to see the comfort of the suburbs as a cheap substitute for the comforts of Jesus. I want you to learn to rely on Jesus in your difficulties rather than running from them. I want you to disconnect your self-worth from your net worth so that you are free to listen to your Lord. I want you to grow spiritually during your time in the city. Don't settle for anything less!

When your whole world is colored by the grace Jesus has shown you, then you will be free. You will be free to follow Him to the global cities of the world with the message of His mercy, forgiveness, and love. You will be free to chase Him back home to fearlessly share about God's love with your family and childhood friends. Or maybe, you'll be free to follow Him into the city long-term.

Epilogue
LONG-TERM LIVING

For those intrepid souls who choose to live in the city long-term, there are a host of issues you must face in order to thrive. If you feel God leading you to consider staying in the city longer, what might that look like?

This chapter works differently than the others. It is a collection of practical wisdom hard-won in the trenches of Boston. For this chapter, I have collaborated with my wife, Heather, because we are partners in life and ministry and because figuring out how to thrive long-term in the city has been largely due to her influence.

COMMUNITY IN A TRANSIENT CHURCH

The beauty of church is that you can become close friends with people you wouldn't normally hang out with. There is a bond. There is a closeness that develops beyond normal relationships. This is no surprise when Christian relationships are built on vulnerability, accountability, and the truth of God's Word.

The danger and difficulty of staying is having close relationship after close relationship ripped out of your life. The temptation is for your heart to harden after you've been hurt. You might keep new people at arm's length or choose to not get too invested in people who will only leave you again. After several years, I was able to label what my wife and I were struggling with as grief. We weren't losing friends to death. We were losing friends to distance, but we were still losing friends.

The three practices which have helped Heather and I keep a soft heart in the midst of such loss are saying goodbye, grieving loss, and developing a long-term community.

When lots of people leave your life, you need to get very good at saying goodbye. The encouraging news is that in the kingdom of God there is no "goodbye forever" there is only "goodbye for now." If you are avoiding goodbyes because of the loss and pain it brings up, you will crumble. You need to learn to say goodbye well. This includes:

- talking directly to those who are leaving about their future plans
- saying thank you for specific things
- considering what gifts to give to departing friends
- making concrete but realistic plans for future communication
- praying together
- blessing people as they leave

If you are a crazy-busy person, this probably seems extravagant. Or perhaps, like me, you tend to live in the future rather than in the past, so you move on from relationships before they are even really over. Saying goodbye well is a skill, and it keeps your heart healthy. Jesus spent quite a bit of time with His disciples giving them the final instructions and final prayer (John 14-17). It was His farewell address. He was saying goodbye. It's interesting that the Bible records for us pages and pages of Jesus saying goodbye.

Once your friends actually leave, you need to give yourself space and time to live with the loss. You have to grieve. I'm not a feeler; I'm a thinker and a doer. The pace of the losses in the city helped change that for me. God softened my heart by putting me in a situation where I would have to learn how to grieve in a godly way or else I would crumble.

Pastor Pete Scazzero, author of *Emotionally Healthy Spirituality,* talks about the steps of godly grief from the story of David in the Bible.[12] I have found his teaching on this to be unbelievably helpful. The progression of godly grief is:

- I pay attention to it.
- I wait in the confusing in between.
- I let the old birth the new.

I remember several summers when Heather and I would both say, "I don't know how many more times we can do this." It is so hard to invest in people only to watch them leave. Making the decision to learn how to grieve well changed that for us. It's still hard, but now Christ is right in the center of our loss, and He walks us through it.

---

[12] "Enlarge Your Soul Through Grief and Loss," Pete Scazzero Sermons, accessed October 7, 2020, https://emotionallyhealthy.libsyn.com/enlarge-your-soul-through-grief-and-loss.

The third practice which has helped to keep my heart soft in the midst of all the loss is developing a long-term community. I participate in a small group at our church because I believe in group life. I love those people and invest in them. I also know most of them will leave in a year or two. So Heather and I decided to invest in people we knew would be around longer.

Right as we were praying and talking about our need for this, my friend, Pastor Charlie Dunn from Hub Church, called us up and suggested a once-per-month dinner for four couples and their kids. This prompted us to start getting together with a couple of city families, plus Justin Gottlieb's family from 7 Mile Road Church. (Justin is from way out in the suburb of Malden, but we let him ride his horse and buggy into town to join us because of his sense of humor, his superb taste in beer, and his excellent beard.)

The group was an answer to a prayer we had barely placed on our lips. We don't study the Bible together, but we do live in biblical community. We invest time and money into these relationships, because we need stability to thrive. These friendships are life-giving and help us follow Jesus in the city. When you need people who are going to be around for a while, you need to actively seek them out, and you need to invest money and time in them.

I've also personally found community in the group of pastors who serve in the city in Boston (our City Guys). We have a brotherhood in Boston committed to helping people live out their faith in Jesus in an urban context. I couldn't do what I do without them because I'm too weak, too prone to sin, and too quick to stray, but they bring me back to God's grace over and over again. You need people like that in your life in the city.

SCHOOLING

Getting an excellent education for your kids in the city is quite simple. Just pay $50k to $60k per year per child for the elite private school in town. If that is a bit out of reach for you, then I'm sorry to say it won't be simple to find what you want. Schooling and education are likely to be a complicated issue in your city household. You've got three common routes when it comes to schooling.

Public schools are the first option and might work for you depending on your location. On the other hand, public schools may offer a completely unacceptable educational experience for your kids, which is more likely. On the negative side of public schooling, various parts of the curricula often seem suspiciously like progressive indoctrination rather than anything remotely resembling an education of classical, liberal ideas.

The positive side of public schooling is that children do not grow up in a bubble. Heather and I had a deep desire to send our children to public schools so we could build relationships with our neighbors and teach our children to live as a light in our city. We also want to expose our children to enough of the world that they learn to interact with those far from God in a winsome way. We want them to see what the world offers and the ways in which it leads to death. We want them to know what their Muslim neighbors believe, and that Jesus loves Muslims too. Public schooling can help facilitate all of this.

Private schools are the second option. Many schools will hold beliefs that you won't agree with, and this will become a problem as your children age. However, other private schools may line up with your beliefs. At first, we thought this would lead to the bubble mentality forming in our kids. Our experience, which may be particular to the Northeast, is that Christian schools are full of non-Christians who want a better education than the public schools can provide, and they provide ample opportunities to build relationships with people far from God.

The third option is home educating your kids. The stigma of home schooling diminishes in the city. It's just as likely for the hipsters in your town to home-educate their kids as the Christians. Or maybe they'll "un-school" them. Heather and I were forced into this route by the coronavirus pandemic. Home schooling is not for everyone. It can diminish your opportunities to build relationships with people in the community, but if it's right for your family, it can be a great option.

When it comes to schooling, I wish there were easy answers. Unfortunately, there are not. I do want to encourage you to make your child's education a matter of prayer and sacrifice. Pray because you are going to need God's intervention. Sacrifice because following Jesus means seeing children as little people to be loved and served through the wise exercise of authority rather than an add-on to complete a picture-perfect life. Jesus actually said that showing love to children is showing love to Him, which is showing love to God.

"Whoever welcomes one of these little children in my name welcomes me; and whoever welcomes me does not welcome me but the one who sent me" (Mark 9:37 NIV).

In our family, this has meant Heather staying home to educate our kids. It has also meant living frugally as an investment in our children and their education. We are sacrificing earning potential to develop the God-potential in our children. This, in turn, makes many women suspicious that Heather has sacrificed her personal potential and reinforced the patriarchy, but we aren't living to impress them. We're following Jesus. In your family, it may look different, but if prayer and sacrifice characterize your decision making, that's a great start.

HOUSING

When you live in a major city, the sticker shock for a tiny apartment can make you faint. It shifts back and forth, but in 2019 Boston was the fourth most expensive city in the U.S. I once put a deposit on an apartment lease that was more than the down payment on my first house in North Carolina. Many people in the city regularly spend 50 percent of their income on housing, particularly people who make less money.

This has led to creative solutions for those people who are following Jesus in the city. We often see people choose to live in community with other Jesus followers. Christians will rent an entire house with five or six bedrooms that they rent out to other

Christians. These homes often have weekly gatherings for dinner or Bible studies and offer a very high level of connection for singles. The support people of faith provide for one another in the city is remarkable when most people live over two hours from their family.

We know of many families who have taken advantage of first-time homebuyer programs and affordable housing programs. We know families who have sold their affordable housing condos to other Christians involved in brining Jesus to the city. Christians also choose to live in houses or units next to one other to provide the support needed to live in the city long-term.

By far, the most common solution to the cost of housing is the least innovative or exciting. It's the side-hustle, and it seems like everyone in the city has one. I used to drive for Uber, which was a great way to get insight into what people really think, but it was an exhausting way to make money. I had kids, so I had to take all the car seats out and vacuum the car before I went out for the night. Then when I got home at 2 a.m., I had to put all the car seats back so everything was ready for my wife when she woke up. I once started a vending machine business (don't do it, they're all scams). I tried to start a podcast. I used to do college prep tutoring. I've done it all.

The side-hustle is not a particularly novel solution, but I always came back to this verse which has grounded me during those times when I was tempted to whine to God and assume I could come up with a better plan for my life:

"Anyone who has been stealing must steal no longer, but must work, doing something useful with their own hands, that they may have something to share with those in need" (Eph. 4:28 NIV).

I'm reminded of this verse not because I used to steal, but because it reminds me that hard work gets me to the point where I have something to share with my family, my friends, and those in need.

I don't mind cleaning toilets if I know it's for the Lord and those I love.

When you think about housing, just know that there will likely be compromises. Perfect only exists for the wealthiest families. We all would do well to remember that what we sacrifice to live in the city is miniscule compared to what those who have come before us have sacrificed to get the gospel to the nations. Some dreams might have to die in the city, but it's ok. God replaces them with better dreams.

REACHING LONG-TERM RESIDENTS

When Heather and I moved to Boston, we began making friends with a group of people who already knew and loved each other. We found one of them was a serious follower of Jesus who had been sharing her faith with the group for years. She was once watching TV on election night together with a bunch of neighbors when the person on television made a passing reference to a "prodigal son." No one in the room knew exactly what it meant, so she explained to them about God's heart toward His run-away kids. They had never heard about it before.

When we spoke to her later about the spiritual state of our friends and neighbors, she made a statement that has stuck with me to this day. "Guys," she said, "this is crockpot evangelism." For those of you who don't know, a crockpot is an Instant Pot before technology happened. It's the opposite of a microwave. Instead of heating things up for three or four minutes, you heat things up for three or four hours. It takes time, it's slow, but the result is worth it.

When we engage with long-term residents, it's crockpot evangelism. It's slow, painstaking work. It can take years of being with people to earn the right to share about Jesus, but the result is worth it.

A WORD OF HOPE

I don't know what dream will have to die for you to live in a city long-term, but I know you will have to sacrifice something. There will probably not be a single-family home with a white picket fence. You may never have that man-cave or she-shed. Much of this book was written underneath my son's bunk bed because I don't have a home office. It's not what I was dreaming of professionally when I would be almost forty.

In the place of those suburban dreams, in place of the American dream, God gives us better dreams. I am excited about the chance to impact global cities for Christ. I wonder what God might do or which city might spark the next revival? Our world is more connected than ever; maybe it won't be a national revival, but a global one.

Living in cities long-term is hard, there's no doubt about that, but we serve a God who is bigger than the city. He walks with us through the most difficult seasons, and He sustains us with His presence. In the city, you'll have difficulties and challenges, but take heart.

"I have told you these things, so that in me you may have peace. In this world you will have trouble. But take heart! I have overcome the world" (John 16:33 NIV).

ACKNOWLEDGEMENTS

As this is my first published book, I would first like to thank my wife, Heather. You are my best friend and the reason I now give different advice to single people looking for someone to marry. I tell them all, "find someone godly, hardworking, honest, and loyal" because you have been that and more in my life. You let me put headphones in to escape from the children for untold hours to learn how to write and publish because you believe in this work we're doing. We are a team. What one of us accomplishes, we both accomplish together.

Thank you to the people of Renewal Church. You've put up with a very dry sense of humor for eight long years. More importantly, you've taught me how beautiful singleness can be, how generous young people can be, and inspired me with your drive to impact global cities for Christ.

To Terry O'Regan: you have the spiritual gifts of encouragement and leadership, a potent combination. You often saw things in me I did not yet see in myself. You believed first, best, and most deeply. Thank you for making this book possible.

Nicole Monteleone, you deserve a jewel in your crown in heaven just for suffering through listening to me talk about this book for hours on end. This book could not have been written before you came to Renewal. Your steadfast dedication to our shared work has allowed me to multiply our combined efforts by putting what we've learned together down on paper. Thank you for serving the Lord with me.

Thank you to Duncan Weachock, the world's most kingdom-minded (and skilled) graphic designer for putting up with my speculations, theories, and never-ending requests about cover design.

A very special thank you to David Butler, an early supporter of this work who listened to the earliest conception of this book by Jamaica Pond. Your steadfast support and encouragement have helped me to last in the city and, hopefully, contribute to God's kingdom work with this book.

Thank you to everyone on the Launch Team who took a risk on an unknown author. I appreciate the time you spent reading advanced copies, writing thoughtful reviews, and spreading the word. This book would exist, but no one on earth but my mom would know about it without you.

Finally, I would like to thank my mom and dad. Your commitment to one another provided the firmest foundation from which myself and my beloved, yet over-achieving, sister have stridden forth into the world. Your belief in me helped me to believe in myself, and I'm forever indebted to your love and generosity.

AUTHOR'S NOTE

I appreciate you reading. The idea for this book came out of an epic eleven-hour, nonstop road trip. My wife, Heather, and I were bored and bemoaning the lack of good resources for young, urban Christians. We wanted something we could put into the hands of every person who walked through the doors of our church and say, "Here, this will get you moving in the right direction."

Because that resource didn't exist, we decided to co-write it. Then after a few months, because we value staying married, we un-decided to co-write it. So most of this book was written during the COVID quarantine of 2020 at a tiny desk underneath my son's loft bed.

It would mean a lot to me if you joined my reader community. You'll get the exclusive City Faith Bonus Pack, plus the free group discussion guide. Get those downloads here:

www.JaredKirk.com/CityFaithBonus

And do leave a review.

They help me and help other readers.

ABOUT THE AUTHOR

Fact. Jared Kirk is an Eagle Scout with a degree in Biomedical Engineering with only one letter in his middle name. (Email me if you think you know it...)

If you are looking for a more helpful bio, look elsewhere. Jared is ethnically Jewish which explains his debonair good looks, his sense of humor, and the pressure from his mother that eventually drove him to write this book. He was chosen twice. The first time, as a part of God's chosen people the Jews, and the second time before the foundation of the world (which was really the first time, chronologically). He lives in Boston, Massachusetts where he leads Renewal Church, sails, teaches, writes, drinks coffee, and searches endlessly for decent Mexican food, but not all at the same time.

Learn more about Jared:

www.JaredKirk.com/about

Sign up for City Faith Insiders and get your free

City Faith Bonus Pack.

www.JaredKirk.com/CityFaithBonus

Made in the USA
Middletown, DE
20 December 2021